The Goths

The Goths

Conquerors of the Roman Empire

Simon MacDowall

Pen & Sword
MILITARY

First published in Great Britain in 2017 by
Pen & Sword Military
an imprint of
Pen & Sword Books Ltd
47 Church Street
Barnsley
South Yorkshire
S70 2AS

ISBN 978-1-47383-764-5

A CIP catalogue record for this book is available from the British Library

Printed and bound in Malta by Gutenberg Press Ltd.

Pen & Sword Books Ltd incorporates the Imprints of Pen & Sword Aviation,
Pen & Sword Maritime, Pen & Sword Military, Wharncliffe Local History,
Pen and Sword Select, Pen and Sword Military Classics, Leo Cooper,
Remember When, Seaforth Publishing and Frontline Publishing.

For a complete list of Pen & Sword titles please contact
PEN & SWORD BOOKS LIMITED
47 Church Street, Barnsley, South Yorkshire, S70 2AS, England
E-mail: enquiries@pen-and-sword.co.uk
Website: www.pen-and-sword.co.uk

Contents

List of Plates

Maps

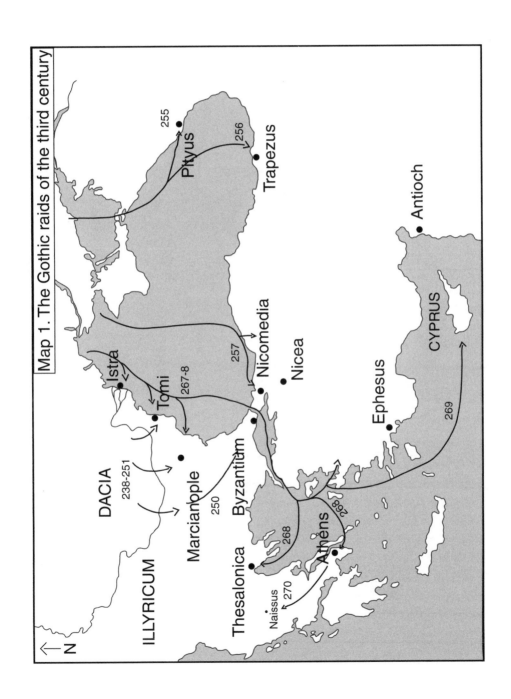

Map 1. The Gothic raids of the third century

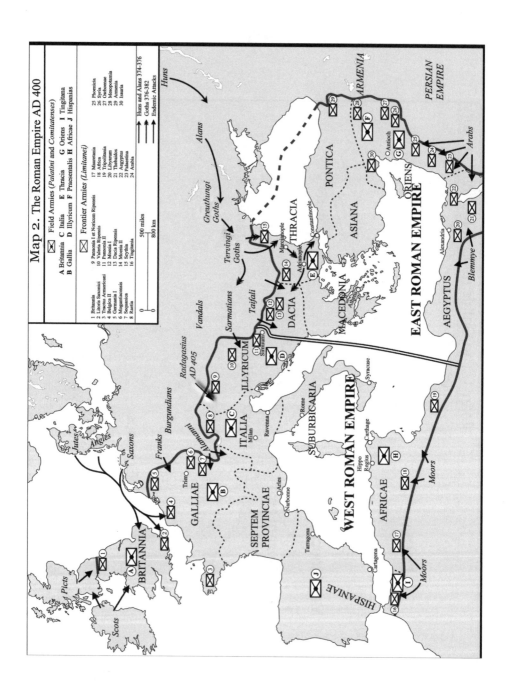

Map 2. The Roman Empire AD 400

Field Armies (*Palatini and Comitatenses*)
A Britannia C Italia   E Thracia   G Oriens   I Tingitana
B Gallia   D Illyricum F Praesentalis H Africae J Hispanias

Frontier Armies (*Limitanei*)

1 Britannia	9 Pannonia I et Noricum Ripensis	17 Mauretania	25 Phoenicia
2 Litora Saxonici	10 Valeria Ripensis	18 Africa	26 Syria
3 Tractus Armoricani	11 Pannonia II	19 Tripolitania	27 Osrhoenae
4 Belgica II	12 Moesia I	20 Libyarum	28 Mesopotamia
5 Germania I	13 Dacia Ripensis	21 Thebaidos	29 Armenia
6 Maguntiacensis	14 Moesia II	22 Aegyptus	30 Isauria
7 Sequanica	15 Scythia	23 Palaestina	
8 Raetia	16 Tingitania	24 Arabia	

500 miles
800 km

Huns and Alans 374-376
Goths 376-382
Endemic Attacks

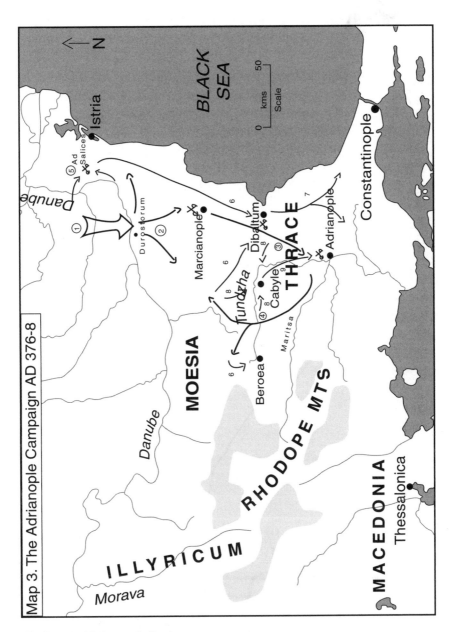

Map 3. The Adrianople Campaign AD 376-8

1   The first wave of Goths cross the Danube
2   The Goths break out of their containment area
3   After winning the Battle of Marcianople Fritigern's followers head south towards Adrianople
4   Failing to capture Adrianople the Tervingi break up into small groups and spread out
5   Huns and Alans reinforce the Goths at Ad Salices
6   The Goths break through the Roman troops which had been bottling them up along the Danube and in the Balkans
7   Bands of Goths spread out through the Thracian countryside
8   Small Gothic Bands converge on Cabyle
9   The march to Adrianople
    Battle sites are marked with crossed swords

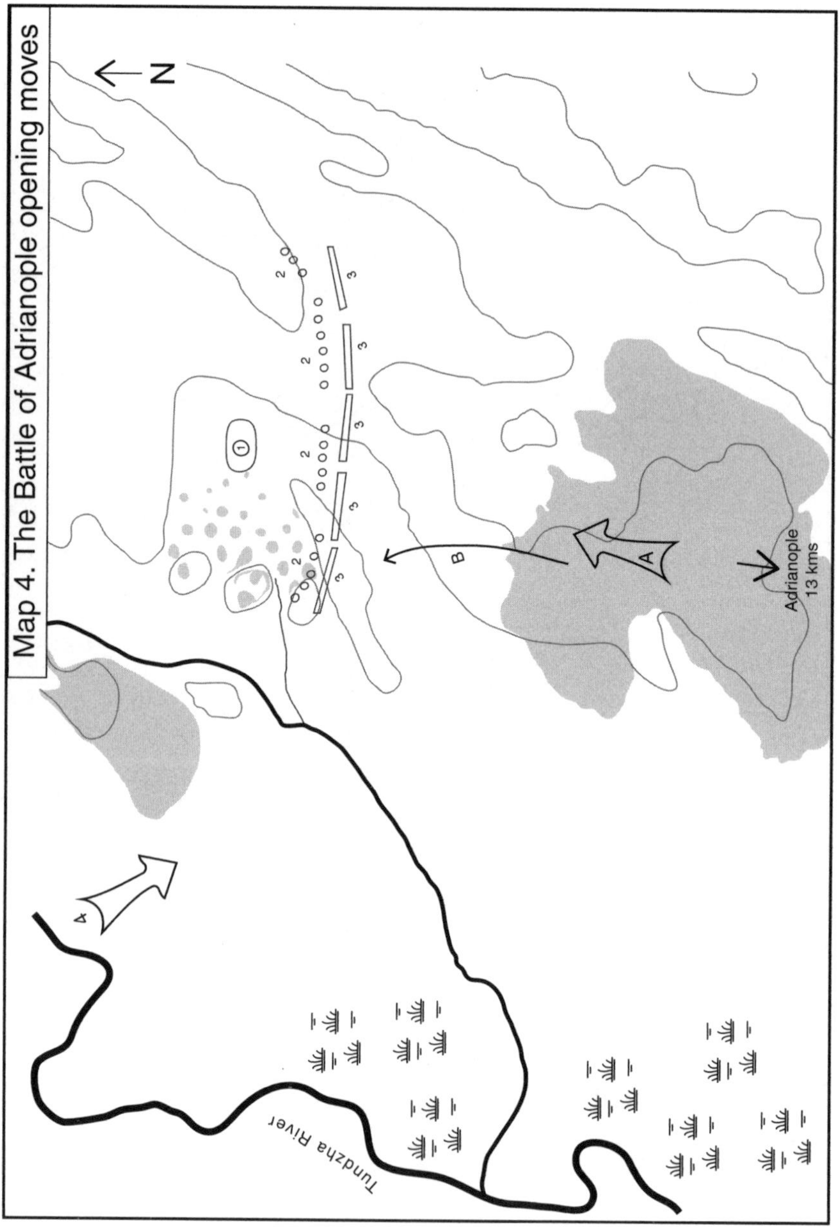

Map 4. The Battle of Adrianople opening moves

1   Centre of the Gothic camp
2   Wagon barricade protecting vulnerable access points to the camp
3   Tervingi warriors deployed on foot
4   Greuthungi and Alan warriors arriving on horseback

A   The Roman army advances along the ridge from Adrianople
B   Roman cavalry supported by archers probe the Gothic position, engaging without authorisation.

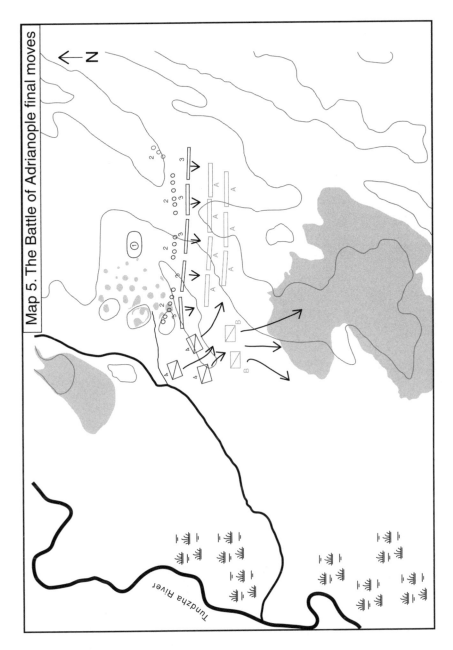

Map 5. The Battle of Adrianople final moves

1   Centre of the Gothic camp
2   Wagon barricade protecting vulnerable access points to the camp
3   Tervingi warriors attack the Roman infantry who have deployed facing them
4   Greuthungi and Alan warriors drive off the Roman cavalry and hit the flank of the infantry

A   Roman infantry
B   Roman cavalry

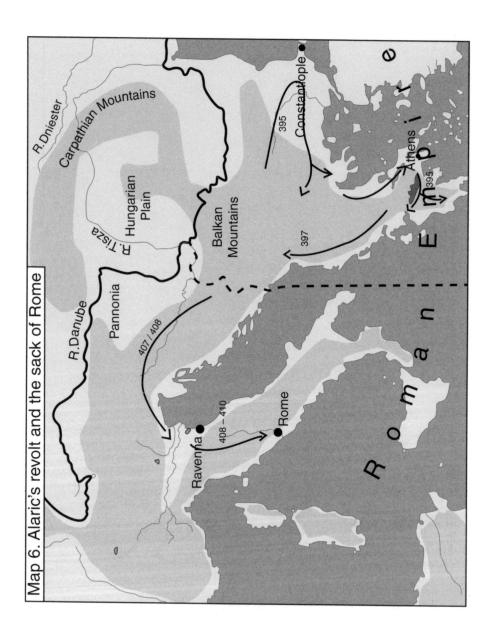

Map 6. Alaric's revolt and the sack of Rome

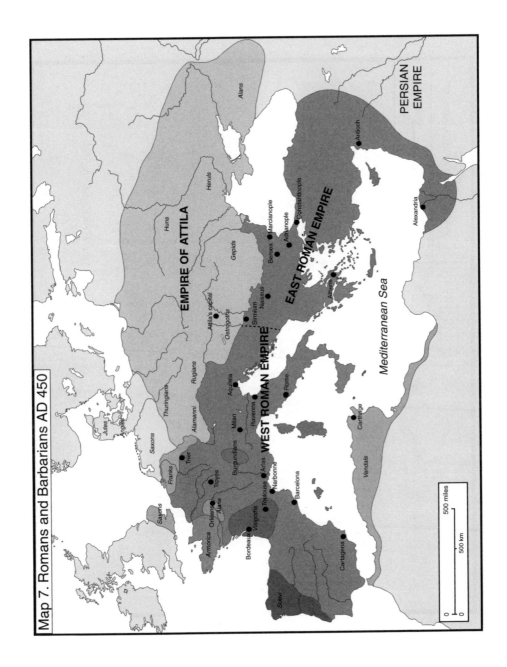

Map 7. Romans and Barbarians AD 450

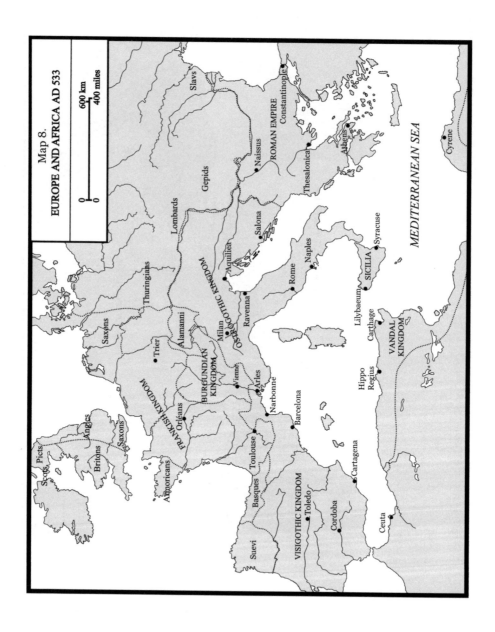

Map 8.
EUROPE AND AFRICA AD 533

0   600 km
0   400 miles

Scots
Picts
Angles
Saxons
Britons
Armoricans
FRANKISH KINGDOM
Trier
Orléans
BURGUNDIAN KINGDOM
Vienne
Arles
Narbonne
Toulouse
Basques
VISIGOTHIC KINGDOM
Toledo
Cordoba
Cartagena
Ceuta
Stuevi
Barcelona
Hippo Regius
Carthage
VANDAL KINGDOM
Lilybaeum
SICILIA
Syracuse
Naples
Rome
Ravenna
OSTROGOTHIC KINGDOM
Milan
Aquileia
Salona
Alamanni
Thuringians
Saxons
Lombards
Gepids
Slavs
Naissus
ROMAN EMPIRE
Constantinople
Thessalonica
Athens
Cyrene
MEDITERRANEAN SEA

Map 9. The War for Italy AD 535-554

Major Engagements

A. Salona
B. Tarbesium
C. Faventia
D. Mugello
E. Ancona (Sea Battle)

F. Siege of Rome
G. Castilinum
H. Siege of Naples
I. Mons Lactarius
J. Taginae

Chapter 1

First Contact

The Goths burst onto the Roman world in the third century AD. Over the following half a millennium they helped to bring about the collapse of the Roman Empire in the West and shape medieval Europe. They destroyed several Roman armies, killed two emperors, propped up several others, sacked Rome, and in the end carved out kingdoms for themselves in France, Italy and Spain. It was not until the 8th century that the last Gothic kingdom was finally destroyed by the Arabs.

Today their name is more familiar to us for things they actually had no part in. The first Gothic cathedrals were constructed long after the Goths were no more. What we now call 'Gothic' architecture acquired its name during the Renaissance as a pejorative term employed by Italians who thought the style to be barbaric. Gothic novels describe dark happenings often located in gothic-style medieval churches or castles; while the black-clad youths who today call themselves 'goths' have nothing in common with the original bearers of that name.

So who were the actual Goths?

Like most of the conquerors of Rome they were a Germanic people. The sixth century historian Jordanes, who was himself of Gothic descent, wrote a history of the Goths which has survived. The oral traditions of the Goths are preserved by Jordanes telling of a slow migration from Scandinavia to modern Poland and then down to the Black Sea.

'Now from this island of Scandza, as from a hive of races or a womb of nations, the Goths are said to have come forth long ago under their King Berig. As soon as they disembarked from their ships and set foot on the land, they straightway gave their name to the place. And even to-day it is said to be called Gothiscandza. Soon they moved from here to the abodes of the Ulmerugi, who then dwelt on the shores of Ocean, where they pitched camp, joined battle with them and drove them from their homes. Then they subdued their neighbours, the Vandals, and thus added to their victories. But when the number of the people increased greatly and Filimer, son of Gadaric, reigned as king — about the fifth since Berig — he decided that the army of the Goths with their families should move from that region. In search of suitable homes and pleasant places they came to the land of Scythia, called Oium in that tongue. Here they were delighted with the great richness of the country... This part of the Goths, which is said to have ...entered with Filimer into the country of Oium, came into possession of the desired land, and there they soon came upon the race of the Spali, joined battle with them and won the victory. Thence the victors hastened to the farthest part of Scythia, which is near the Sea of Pontus [The Black Sea]. For so the story is generally told in their early songs... We read that on their first migration the Goths dwelt in the land of Scythia near Lake Maeotis [The Azov Sea]. On the second migration they went to Moesia, Thrace and Dacia [modern Bulgaria and Romania] and after their third they dwelt again in Scythia, above the Sea of Pontus'.

For many years archaeologists have sought to either confirm or disprove the pre-historic migration of the Goths and other Germans from Scandinavia into central Europe and then further south. Similar artefacts found from the Baltic to the Black Sea could confirm the Gothic oral history and in the 19th century this was more or less accepted. Modern studies have been less believing. Although archaeological finds do tend to confirm a population shift from what is now Poland to the Black Sea, the links to Scandinavia are far more tenuous. This has led some historians to doubt a migration from Scandinavia ever took place.

There are etymological links between the Goths and Scandinavia. Gotland in modern Sweden is the most obvious and could indicate an original Gothic home-land from which some, but not all, Goths migrated in the centuries before the birth of Christ. Ptolemy mentions a tribe called the *Goutai* living in Scandinavia during the second century AD but we must wonder how much firsthand informa-tion he had of such a faraway place.

Modern archaeology has neither proved nor disproved the oral tradition of the Gothic Scandinavian homeland as recounted by Jordanes. It has, however, con-firmed a distinctive culture amongst a group of peoples living in the Vistula basin in the first two centuries AD. It is known to archaeologists as the *Wielbark cul-ture* named after the village in Pomerania where many graves and stone circles have been found which have been tentatively attributed to the early Goths. The distinctive artefacts in this region increase in density, gradually spreading further south along the Vistula from the Baltic until the second century AD. Then they tail off as new, yet similar, finds show up to the north of the Black Sea — called the *Cernjachov culture* by archaeologists. There are similarities between the Wielbark and Cernjachov cultures which are markedly different from their neighbours. For example, they did not bury weapons with deceased warriors while the previous inhabitants and some western neighbours did. The decline of the Weilbark and emergence of the Cernjachov finds coincide nicely with the literary accounts of the migration of the Goths from central Europe to the Black Sea. Some modern historians cite this as corroboration of Jordanes' migratory account while others dismiss any connection.

So what does all this tell us about the early Goths? Without conclusive evidence to the contrary I am inclined to accept the oral tradition of the Goths which has some of their ancestors moving from modern Sweden to modern Poland probably around the second century BC. Merging with and displacing original inhabitants they established settlements along the Vistula River and remained in that region until sometime in the second century AD when, under Filimer's leadership, some of them migrated further south to the shores of the Black Sea and the lower Danube. The extensive areas of the Weilbark and Cernjachov cultures were not exclusively Gothic but the Goths shared similar cultural traits with many other tribes in the same regions.

As the sixth century Roman historian Procopius recounts:

> 'There were many Gothic nations in earlier times, just as also at the present, but the greatest and most important of all are the Goths, Vandals, Visigoths, and Gepids… All these, while they are distinguished from one another by their names, as has been said, do not differ in anything else at all. For they all have white bodies and fair hair, and are tall and handsome to look upon, and they use the same laws and practise a common religion. For they are all of the Arian faith, and have one language called Gothic; and, as it seems to me, they all came originally from one tribe, and were distinguished later by the names of those who led each group. This people used to dwell above the Ister [Danube] River from of old'.

Scope and Sources

This book tells the story of the Goths who, perhaps more than any other Germanic barbarians, shaped the events that led to the fall of the Roman Empire in the West. It is primarily a military history, examining how the Goths fought both for and against the Romans; how they managed to destroy the Emperor's army at Adrianople; establish a new contract between Romans and barbarians; carve out kingdoms for themselves inside the Empire; and their eventual demise. All of this will be placed in the political, economic and social context of the times.

The book is aimed at the general reader with an interest in the military aspects of the barbarian conquests of Rome rather than the academic specialist. In recent years there have been a number of excellent academic books about the Goths, most notably those written by Peter Heather. Those wishing to delve deeper into the story of the Goths would do well to consult them. There have also been many new modern investigations of the fall of the West Roman Empire and late Roman warfare. Many of these have been very helpful in placing the story of the Goths in a wider political context. I have listed the most useful ones in the bibliography.

Unlike the Vandals, covered by the first book in this series, we have relatively plentiful information about the Goths. Jordanes, a Romano-Gothic historian wrote the *Getica* — a history of the Goths in the mid sixth century as a summary of the now lost twelve volume History of the Goths by Cassiodorus, a Roman senator who served Theodoric the Ostrogoth in the sixth century. Much of what Jordanes wrote has to be taken with a grain of salt as he was at pains to glorify the deeds of his Gothic audience. Much like a modern British tabloid journalist he would not necessarily let the facts get in the way of a good story yet he does preserve Gothic oral history and he presents us with a view of the world as the Goths would have recognized it. Some of Cassiodorus' letters, written on behalf of Theodoric also survive, giving us a unique insight into relations between Goths and Romans in sixth century Italy.

All other contemporary accounts come from the Goths' Roman enemies. Of these, the writings of Ammianus Marcellinus and Procopius are the most interesting and complete. The first was a Roman military officer turned historian who wrote his history of the Roman Empire around 395. He describes in detail the first migration of the Goths into Roman territory and their victory over the Romans at the Battle of Adrianople in 378. As a soldier himself he had firsthand knowledge of what ancient battle was like and he lived through the events he described. Although he at times drifts off into poetic licence he does give us a great deal of detail about the Gothic-Roman conflict towards the end of the fourth century. Procopius, secretary to the East Roman general Belisarius, gives similar firsthand information at the other end of the Gothic story. Writing in the mid-sixth century, at more or less the same time as Jordanes, he describes in detail the war between the Ostrogoths and Romans in Italy. He was actually present at many of the events he described, including the year-long Gothic siege of Rome in 537-8. Although obviously biased, Procopius's account is reasonably balanced. His descriptions of the battles and the various political machinations are both realistic and reliable.

We have much less information about the Goths in the early years of their interaction with Rome before 376 and the same is true for the middle part of their story in the fifth century. In both cases we have to content ourselves with brief snippets — often only a line or two about a major battle without any details of what went on or the composition of the armies.

One source which does give us some idea of the Roman armies of the time is the *Notitia Dignitatum*. This is a list of offices and army units from the end of the fourth century in the east and early fifth century in the west. This tells us the official orders of battle of the Roman army close to the time of the Gothic sack of Rome. While it needs to be treated with a fair degree of caution it is invaluable in building a picture of the Roman army and political structure in the late fourth-early fifth centuries. At this time the Empire was divided in two. The Western Empire was ruled at first from Milan and then in the fifth century from Ravenna. The city of Rome was still the most important city in the West but it had ceased to be the seat of power during the reign of Diocletian at the end of the third century. The Eastern Empire was ruled from Constantinople and it continued to survive for another millennium after the fall of the West.

Enemies of Rome

In the first centuries AD the Goths were relatively unknown to the Romans although they are mentioned by Tactius, who wrote about the Germanic tribes of the first century AD. He places them living to the east of the Vistula in modern Poland. 'Beyond the Lugii are the Gothones, who are governed by kings. Their rule is somewhat more autocratic than in the other German states but not to the degree that freedom is destroyed'. This would more or less tally with Jordanes' account of where the Goths lived on the shores of the Baltic Sea before moving further south and east. The Lugii may be associated with the Vandals and if so Tacitus is consistent with Jordanes' account of the Goths being neighbours of the Vandals in their early years.

The early Goths were far from the Roman frontiers and busy holding their own against neighbouring tribes. When they moved southeast towards the Black Sea this began to change.

'Now the Gothic race gained great fame in the region where they were then dwelling, that is in the Scythian land on the shore of Pontus, holding undisputed sway over great stretches of country, many arms of the sea and many river courses. By their strong right arm the Vandals were often laid low, the Marcomanni held their footing by paying tribute and the princes of the Quadi were reduced to slavery'. (Jordanes)

In the second century AD something, we do not know what, caused a south-ern movement of several German tribes from their central European home-lands. The Asding Vandals moved from modern Silesia into Bohemia, pressing up against the lands held by the Marcomanni and Quadi. At the same time Filimer's Goths moved down to the Black Sea. Jordanes also says that there was another Gothic migration into the regions of the lower Danube. These migra-tions squeezed the Marcomanni, Quadi and Sarmatians who occupied the lands on the Roman Danube frontier and probably sparked off the Marcomannic wars (166-180 AD).

Marcus Aurelius eventually defeated the tribes that spilled over the Danube frontier. As far as we know the Goths took no part in the conflict with Rome at this time. The archaeological record shows a shift from the former homelands of the Goths in northern Poland to the south at the same time as the onset of the Marcomannic wars. From this we can conclude that it was the southern migration of the Goths and others that sparked off the war with Rome in a foreshadowing of the famous Hun migrations to follow.

By the early part of the third century AD the Goths were occupying the north-western coast of the Black Sea and the lands just beyond the lower Danube frontier. According to Jordanes they increased their power at the expense of neighbouring tribes.

It would be wrong to think of the Goths at this time as a powerful entity united under a single ruler. Rather they were a group of clans sharing a common language and cultural traits. Groups of them might band together on occasion and at other times act alone. Individual chieftains might command a few hundred warriors, only a few of whom would be full time retainers. As a chieftain increased his wealth — often through trade with Rome — he would be able to attract and maintain more full time warriors and consequently increase his power and influence. Defeating a neighbouring tribe and taking prisoners would help but the real prizes were to be won across the frontier. Even the poorest Roman provinces enjoyed far greater wealth and material possessions than any of the tribes beyond the frontier so a successful foray into Roman territory could set up an ambitious Gothic leader for life.

In the 230s, as the various Gothic clans were expanding their power to the north of the Black Sea and on the lower Danube, the Roman Empire was convulsed by civil war. The legions defending the frontiers were drawn off to fight each other providing a perfect opportunity for various energetic Gothic leaders to try their luck at raiding into Roman territory. The first recorded raid took place in 238 when some Goths crossed the lower Danube and sacked a few settlements. Encouraged by this success other bands followed suit.

Jordanes says that the Goths crossed the Danube and ravaged Moesia (Roman territory along the upper Danube) and Thrace (modern Bulgaria and European Turkey). The Emperor Philip (244-249) appointed Decius to lead the Roman counter attack. Decius dismissed those soldiers who had failed to hold the Danube against the Goths and some of these joined forces with a Gothic leader whom Jordanes calls King Ostrogotha. This name, with its ties to the later Ostrogoths, is probably anachronistic and it is highly unlikely that the Goths at this time had any single ruler.

'Having as allies for this war some of the Taifali and Astringi and also 3,000 of the Carpi, a race of men very ready to make war and frequently hostile to the Romans. …He (Ostrogotha) placed in command Argaithus and Guntheric, the noblest leaders of his race. They speedily crossed the Danube, devastated Moesia a second time and approached Marcianople, the famed metropolis of that land. Yet after a long siege they departed, upon receiving money from the inhabitants'. (Jordanes)

It is interesting to note that Jordanes is quite clear that the Gothic invaders were a multi-ethnic force, probably including Roman deserters. This was a pattern which would be followed in many years to come. The Taifali were related to the Goths and had occupied territory to the west of the Goths on the lower Danube. The Astringi could refer to the Asding Vandals although such an alliance seems unlikely as for most part the Goths and Vandals were in conflict with each other. The Carpi were the original inhabitants of Dacia (modern Romania) who had remained beyond Roman control and who were eventually absorbed or displaced by the Goths.

It is likely that the Goths and others who raided across the Danube between 238 and 250 were a number of individual bands numbering in the low thousands at best. Most probably they operated independently rather than under a single command. They would strike swiftly to amass loot and captives, then cross back over the Danube before they could be caught by the Romans. As far as we can tell there were no major engagements between the Goths and Romans but there must have been many skirmishes of which the Romans seem usually to have had the upper hand. By 249 Decius felt successful enough to proclaim himself emperor and march on Italy to overthrow Philip.

In 250 Cniva, another Gothic leader, crossed the Danube, ravaged the Balkan provinces, threatened Nicopolis, and then retired to the Balkan mountains when Decius' army approached. Then, as the Romans were resting near Beroea (Stara Zagora in modern Bulgaria), Cniva launched a surprise attack and scattered them. He then moved on to besiege Philippopolis (Plovdiv, Bulgaria), apparently without Decius attempting to relieve the city. After a long siege Julius Priscus, the commander of the garrison, colluded with the Goths, let them have the city and proclaimed himself Emperor. Now needing a decisive victory to shore up his position, Decius took the offensive against Cniva in early 251. The two armies met near Abritus (modern Razgrad, Bulgaria) as Zosimus, a fifth century Greek historian, describes:

'The Scythians, [Goths] taking advantage of the disorder which every-where prevailed through the negligence of Philip, crossed the Tanais, [Don River] and pillaged… Thrace. Decius, marching against them, was not only victorious in every battle, but recovered the spoils they had taken, and endeavoured to cut off their retreat to their own country, intending to destroy them all, to prevent them ever again making a similar incursion. For this purpose he posted Gallus on the bank of the Tanais with a competent force, and led in person the remainder of his army against the enemy. This expedition exceeded to his utmost wish; but Gallus — who was disposed to innovation — sent agents to the barbarians, requesting their concurrence in a conspiracy against Decius. To this they gave a willing assent. Gallus retained his post on the bank of the Tanais, while the barbarians divided themselves into three divisions, the first of which posted itself behind a marsh. Decius having destroyed a considerable number of the first division, the second advanced, which he likewise defeated, and discovered part of the third, which lay near the marsh. Gallus sent intelligence to him, that he might march against them across the fen. Proceeding therefore incautiously in an unknown place, he and his army became entangled in the mire, and under that disadvantage were so assailed by the missiles of the barbarians, that not one of them escaped with life. Thus ended the life of the excellent Emperor Decius'. (Zosimus)

Here Zosimus describes in some detail not only the first major Gothic victory over Roman forces but also the death of an emperor in action against Germanic barbarians. It was the first but not the last time that the Goths would kill a Roman emperor on the field of battle. He also attributes the Roman defeat to treachery on the part of Gallus who then succeeded Decius as emperor. Whenever a major defeat occurred, Roman historians invariably put it down to treachery as any other explanation was simply incomprehensible. That the Goths could have defeated Decius without help seemed beyond belief. Such attributions of Roman treachery to a barbarian victory will occur many times again in the story of the Goths. Although we do need to take such explanations with a grain of salt, as Gallus succeeded Decius as emperor, there could well be some truth in this case.

We have no idea how many troops were involved at the Battle of Abritus (sometimes referred to as the Battle of *Forum Terebronii*) nor the composition of the armies. It is reasonable to assume that as an emperor beset by internal enemies, Decius would have had a reasonably sizeable force — probably something in the region of 15-25,000 men. Anything less than this would have left him very exposed to a frontier commander with Imperial ambitions. Having previously been caught out by the Goths at Beroea, this time he would have wanted to ensure that he had sufficient forces to ensure victory. It would have been very difficult for Cniva to have matched those sort of numbers. His was a group of raiders from many different tribes, eager to get safely back over the Danube with their loot. Even gathering together 10,000 men at one place and time would have been a great undertaking.

This does lead some credence to Zosimus' account of Gallus' treachery. If Gallus commanded a substantial part of the Roman army and then conspired with Cniva, then the actual numbers of troops on each side at Abritus may have been more or less equal — maybe something close to 10,000 men each. It may also be the case that Decius' army had been split into several detachments to chase down separate bands of invaders and that they had not all be able to concentrate together in time to take part in the battle.

The Early Gothic Army

Most of our knowledge of early German warfare comes from Tacitus who wrote several hundred years previously. At that time he tells us that:

> 'Generally speaking, their strength lies in infantry rather than cavalry. So foot soldiers accompany the cavalry into action, their speed on foot being such that they can easily keep up with charging horsemen. The best men are chosen from the whole body of young warriors and placed with the cavalry in front of the main battle line…The battle line is made up of wedge shaped formations. To give ground, provided that you return to the attack, is considered good tactics rather than cowardice'.

When they were living in the Vistula basin the early Goths would probably have fought in a very similar manner with most warriors fighting on foot while a few notable men had horses. Depending on the circumstances, the mounted men might dismount or remain on horseback with agile young men accompanying them on foot. As the Goths moved into the more open terrain of modern southern Ukraine, horses would have become increasingly important to them. Mounting up would have allowed them to range over wider areas while maintaining a substantial horse herd would have been much easier than it had been in the forested hills of central Europe. By the third century it is highly likely that a sizeable proportion of the wealthier Gothic warriors had horses and rode them into battle even if they later dismounted to fight on foot.

The Gothic victory over Decius in 251 was accomplished when the Romans ran into difficulty in boggy ground which was apparently less of an obstacle to the Goths. Therefore it is reasonable to conclude that the Goths in the third century still fought primarily on foot and maybe in looser order than their Roman opponents. The Romans depended on maintaining close formation to fend off attack while the Goths relied on the fighting prowess of individual warriors.

Zosimus also says that the Romans 'were so assailed by the missiles of the barbarians that not one of them escaped with life'. The caricature of a Germanic army of the time is that they relied on hand-to-hand combat only. This passage shows that the Goths understood the value of fighting at a distance with bows or javelins and knew how to use difficult terrain to their advantage. This is a far cry from the typical image of simplistic barbarians without any tactical finesse.

Probably most Gothic warriors carried light javelins in addition to their spears and swords but then so did the Romans. The Roman heavy infantry at this time were also supported by archers, usually deployed on the flanks or shooting overhead from the rear ranks of a heavy infantry formation. For the Goths to have had a missile advantage over their Roman opponents many of the warriors who would normally have fought hand-to-hand must have kept their distance in the last stages of the battle against Decius. Probably they avoided close combat and showered the enemy with javelins and arrows as the legionaries struggled across the boggy ground.

Zosimus tells us that the Romans did manage to defeat the first two divisions of the Gothic army but the third, hidden in ambush, destroyed the Romans when they were literarily bogged down. A ferocious charge into close combat may have been the preferred Gothic tactic but it would seem that they were perfectly prepared to adapt their fighting methods to suit the terrain and circumstances. Certainly many of the Gothic warriors may have been mounted as they approached the battlefield but then they dismounted to fight in the difficult terrain. This became a hallmark of Gothic warfare for many years. Unlike the Romans, who had cavalry fighting on horseback and infantry fighting on foot, the Goths did not make such distinctions. A warrior was a warrior. If he had a horse he would fight on horseback in open terrain or to ride down disordered groups of men. In close country or when fighting on the defensive he would dismount. Likewise a warrior who did not own a horse might mount up once he acquired one to move swiftly from place to place.

Typically the Romans portrayed the Germanic warriors as half naked savages yet archaeology has revealed that the Goths were becoming increasingly good metal workers. After a year of reasonably successful raids, the capture of Philippopolis and their victory at Beroea, Cniva's Goths, Carpi, Roman deserters and others would have supplemented their native equipment from the arsenals and bodies of their enemies. At this time probably most of the men would have had good weapons even if only a few of them had body armour. In the marshes of Abritus any lack of armour would not have been a disadvantage.

Chapter 2

Over Land and Sea

Rome's Crisis

From the third century onwards the story of the Goths becomes inextricably entwined with that of Rome. Roman politics and economics had a profound impact on the Goths causing them to do things which shaped Roman history in turn. The mid third century was a period of terrible upheaval for the Roman Empire. From the assassination of the Emperor Alexander Severus in 235 until the ascension of Diocletian in 284, the Empire was torn apart by civil wars. One general after another was proclaimed emperor by his troops and fought off similar claimants. Most reigned only briefly and at times there were several men carrying the title of 'Augustus', sometimes ruling over different parts of the Empire and at other times fighting each other to control the same territory.

Silver and gold coins were increasingly cut with baser metals as these temporary emperors struggled to find the cash to reward the soldiers on whose support they depended. Hyperinflation was the consequence. Trade routes became unsafe, barter began to replace payment in cash and even taxes were often collected in kind. Infrastructure was neglected as those in power spent all their resources on maintaining an army to fight off rivals.

With Roman armies turned on each other, those peoples living beyond the frontiers saw an opportunity that was too good to pass up. Beyond the Danube and Rhine lay riches beyond their imagination and they were seemingly open for the taking. It can be no coincidence that the first Gothic incursions into Roman territory began in the late 230s at the same time as the Empire began to fall apart. The Goths were not the only ones to take advantage of the situation.

To the east the Sassanid dynasty re-established a vibrant new Persian Empire when they overthrew the Parthians in 224. Under Shapur I, the Sassanids adopted an aggressive policy aimed at diminishing Rome's influence over the border lands between the two empires while extending their own. Until well beyond the end of the Western Empire, Rome and Persia were in a more or less constant state of war. In 260 the Persians destroyed a Roman army, captured the Emperor Valerian and subjected him to humiliating obeisance — the Persian king Shapur apparently using him as a mounting block when he got on and off his horse.

Meanwhile, on the Rhine frontier, the other German tribes were coalescing into larger confederations capable of fielding more warriors with greater resources. They too took advantage of Rome's internal disorder to raid into Gaul (modern France and Belgium) and northern Italy. One band even penetrated as far as northern Spain to sack Tarragona.

Between 235 and 284, there were more than twenty Roman emperors with many other usurpers not quite making it. The *Historia Augusta* names this period as the *Time of the Thirty Pretenders*. Those emperors who reigned for more than a few days had a hierarchy of strategic objectives. The first was to prevent any other Roman general from threatening his position. If he was successful in neutralizing internal opposition then his second priority would be to defend the rich eastern provinces against the Persians. If he was able to do this then perhaps he would devote some resources to protect the Danube and Rhine frontiers from barbarian incursions.

With the benefit of hindsight it is easy for us to criticize Roman policies which saw a usurper as a greater threat than a barbarian invasion. A newly proclaimed emperor, however, was far more likely to lose his power and life at the hands of another usurper than for any other reason. A barbarian invasion might be devastating for the local populace but eventually it would be contained, the barbarians destroyed and a few expeditions into their homelands would cow them into submission. A suitable native leader would be found who could be bribed to keep the peace and provide recruits for the Roman army.

This had been the pattern for centuries. The Marcomannic Wars (166-180 AD) had been the most serious barbarian incursion into Roman territory since the days of the Republic but in the end the outcome was the same. Despite the destruction they caused, the barbarians were defeated by Marcus Aurelius and cowed into accepting Roman hegemony. The defeat and death of the Emperor Decius at the hands of the Goths in 251 was the first indication that the pattern may have been changing. Not for the last time, the Romans attempted to buy off the Goths without first really defeating them.

An Opportunity for Glory

According to Zosimus, the new emperor Gallus permitted Cniva's Goths to return home with their loot and captives after their victory over Decius. He also paid them an annual tribute to keep them quiet. The policy did not work. Emboldened by success the Goths expanded their power at the expense of neighbouring tribes, including those under Roman protection. At the same time a devastating plague swept through Roman lands:

'Gallus was so supine in the administration of the Empire, that the Scythians [Goths] in the first place terrified all the neighbouring nations, and then laid waste all the countries as far as the [Black Sea] coast; not leaving one nation subject to the Romans unpillaged, and taking almost all the unfortified towns, and many that were fortified. Besides the war on every side, which was insupportably burdensome to them, the cities and villages were infested with a pestilence, which swept away the remainder of mankind in those regions; nor was so great a mortality ever known in any former period'. (Zosimus)

In 253, as the Persians invaded the eastern provinces of the Roman Empire, the Goths again burst over the frontiers. As previously, these incursions were conducted by various bands attacking at different times and places rather than by single, coordinated invasion force (see Map 1). The Goths were not alone in taking advantage of the opportunity created by the war between Rome and Persia. Zosimus says that they were joined by the Borani, the Urugundi and the Carpi, while the *Historia Augusta* lists the Tervingi, Greuthungi, Austrogothi, Visi, Gepids, Heruls, Peucini, and Celts.

Some of these names are reasonably accurate, others quite possibly made up. The Tervingi and Greuthungi were Gothic clans who are well attested by others in the following century. The Austrogothi and Visi mentioned in the *Historia Augusta* also clearly refer to Goths. Probably written in the late fourth century, the *Historia Augusta* is not the most reliable of sources and it may be that the authors were simply applying later names to fill gaps in their knowledge. It is worth noting, however, that this part of the *Historia Augusta* was written long before the establishment of the Visigothic and Ostrogothic kingdoms and it would be wrong to assume that these were their direct ancestors. The Roman army in the late fourth century included a unit known as the *Visi*. So it is possible that there was a Gothic clan known by that name even if it had only a vague connection to the later Visigoths.

The Heruls and Gepids were other eastern Germanic tribes and the Heruls certainly took an active part in the war to follow, probably acting on their own rather than in any kind of formal alliance with the Goths. Jordanes tells us that the name of the Heruls came from their homeland around the swamps near Lake Maeotis — called *'hele'* by the Greeks [Asov Sea]. 'They were a people swift of foot... for there was at that time no race that did not choose from them its light-armed troops for battle'. In the centuries to follow the Heruls were always noted for the lightness of their arms in contrast to other Germanic tribes.

According to Jordanes the Gepids were related to the Goths and their name was derived from the Gothic word *gepanta* meaning 'slow': '"Gepanta" signifies something slow and stolid, the word Gepid arose as a gratuitous name of reproach. I do not believe this is very far wrong, for they are slow of thought and too sluggish for quick movement of their bodies'.

We have already seen how the Carpi were involved in earlier raids. Although they were being gradually edged out by the Goths it is quite likely that bands of them would have taken advantage of the general confusion to raid into Roman Dacia from their strongholds in the Carpathian Mountains. This leaves the Borani, Celts, Urugundi and Peucini. The first name is not certain but the term could simply mean 'men from the north' and therefore might include Goths. Celtic tribes had long been displaced so their inclusion in the list is probably meant to hark back to classical times and give a sense of a motley horde of barbarians. According the Jordanes the Peucini were a people from the island of Peuce in the mouth of the Danube while the Urugundi cannot be identified.

Whichever tribes and clans actually took part in the attacks to follow, the picture we have is of a large number of different peoples taking advantage of the chaos in the Roman Empire to seize loot and captives, then return home with their new portable wealth. These were not yet invasions intent on carving out new territory inside the Empire, nor were they coordinated actions of a grand alliance. The individual groups were probably relatively small, often numbering in the hundreds or low thousands. Such groups of men would be able to live off the land with relative ease and would have avoided contact with Roman armies rather than seeking battle. Roman historians typically exaggerated the numbers, presenting us with an image of innumerable hordes of barbarians sweeping across the frontier.

> 'There were then, in fact, 320,000 men of these tribes under arms... What tale has ever imagined, what poet ever conceived such a number? There were 320,000 armed men! Add to these their slaves, add also their families, their wagon-trains, too, consider the streams they drank dry and the forests they burned, and, finally, the labour of the earth itself which carried such a swollen mass of barbarians!' (*Historia Augusta*)

For more than twenty years many different bands of Goths and others spread devastation throughout the Balkans, Greece and Asia Minor. Tens or even hundreds of thousands of barbarians must have been involved at some time or another over these two decades. Therefore it would have seemed like a vast horde to the Romans even if individual bands of raiders may have been relatively small. That said, there were times when the barbarians gathered together larger forces. Cniva could not have defeated Decius unless he had several thousand men under his command and other encounters with Roman armies suggest that there were times when tens of thousands gathered together for a major expedition.

Raiders of the Black Sea

In 253 Aemilianus, the governor of Moesia, defeated a band of Goths on the Danube and then drew off his frontier forces to Italy in a bid to oust Gallus from the Imperial throne. By the end of the year both he and Gallus were dead and Valerian had been proclaimed emperor, appointing his son Gallienus as co-ruler. Meanwhile the Persians invaded Roman Mesopotamia and Syria, sacking the great city of Antioch. Taking advantage of the situation the Goths once again raided across the Danube. Some of them penetrated as far as Macedonia. Zosimus says that the Marcomanni also joined in to attack across the Danube at the same time.

Raids across the upper Danube continued into 254 but we have no details of what happened. At the same time the tribes living along the northern Black Sea coast found a new route to plunder Roman territory. They took to the sea to cross over and raid the north coast of Asia Minor. Zosimus tells us that it was the enigmatic Borani who did this first, appropriating ships from the local inhabitants.

'They easily effected by the aid of those that reside on the Bosphorus, who were induced more through fear than good-will to supply them with vessels, and to guide them in their passage… they yielded to fear, and gave the Scythians a free ingress into Asia, even carrying them over in their own ships'.

The raiders plundered the countryside and attempted to storm the fortified town of Pityus (Pitsunda in modern Abkhasia). They were driven off by a vigorous defence and after suffering heavy casualties they sailed back home. A second attack followed. This time the barbarians struck at Trapezus (Trabazon in modern Turkey), which according to Zosimus, was defended by 10,000 men.

'When they commenced the siege of [Trapezus], they did not therefore even imagine that they should succeed, as it was surrounded by two walls; but when they observed that the soldiers were addicted to sloth and inebriety, and that instead of continuing on guard, they were always in search of pleasures and debauchery, they piled against the wall trees which they had prepared for the purpose of scaling it, on which their troops mounted in the night and took the city. The soldiers within were struck with consternation at the sudden and unexpected assault; some of them succeeded in escaping through the gates; the rest were slaughtered by the enemy. Having thus got possession of the place, the barbarians acquired an incredible quantity of money, besides a very great number of slaves; for almost all the inhabitants of the country had fled for refuge into that city, as it was strongly fortified. Having demolished all the temples and houses, and everything that contributed to the grandeur or ornament of the city, and devastated the adjacent country, they returned home with a great number of ships'. (Zosimus)

We do not know if the Borani were Goths or included Goths. However the success of these initial seaborne raids encouraged others to do the same and they certainly included both Goths and Heruls. We should not think of the Goths as suddenly becoming expert seafarers nor building Viking style longships of their own design. Instead they commandeered fishing boats and trade ships to transport their warriors. Zosimus tells us that the Goths prepared a fleet which was built by Roman captives and others who saw financial opportunity by providing the barbarians with their shipbuilding skills.

The Goths attempted a different seaborne attack from the earlier one conducted by the Borani across the Black Sea. Zosimus says that they waited until winter and then set sail along the north coast towards Byzantium (modern Istanbul) with some of their forces marching overland along the north shore of the Black Sea. Making an agreement with local fishermen, those Goths who had marched overland boarded the fishing boats to join the seaborne warriors to pass through the Bosphorus. Although there was a strong Roman garrison, the troops fled as the barbarians approached, allowing the Gothic amphibious force to capture Chalcedon without opposition (the Kadıköy district of modern Istanbul). There, according to Zosimus, they got possession of an abundance of money, arms, and provisions and then went on to sack several more cities including Nicomedia (modern Izmit) and Nicaea (modern Iznik) before returning home laden with loot.

From 257 until 267 the historical record of Gothic activity on the Danube and Black Sea suddenly goes quiet. Our sources are preoccupied instead either with the monumental struggle between Rome and Persia, or Gallienus' campaigns in Gaul and Italy. We are told that the seaborne raids across and along the Black Sea coast were so devastating that Valerian was diverted from his counter-attack against the Persians to shore up the defences of the region. As the raiders from the north had not suffered any significant defeat we can only assume that the Gothic raids continued even if no primary source confirms this.

By 267 Gallienus was sole emperor, Valerian having being captured by the Persians. Roman armies were busy fighting the Palmyrans in Syria while Gallienus was occupied seeing off multiple usurpers. It is at this point that we learn of a new amphibious invasion of Goths and Heruls. The *Historia Augusta* claims that the invasion was carried out by a highly unlikely 2000 ships. Even if most of these had been commandeered fishing boats it is hardly credible that an armada of even half that size could have been assembled. As far as it is possible to say, several fleets left the north shore of the Black Sea, striking out south and west and passing through the Dardanelles.

> 'There was fighting in Moesia and there were many battles near Marcianopolis... There was fighting, besides, at Byzantium, for those Byzantines who survived acted with courage. There was fighting at Thessalonica, to which the barbarians had laid siege... There was fighting in divers places'. (*Historia Augusta*)

Jordanes has this to say of the invasion of 267/8:

> 'Respa, Veduc and Thuruar, leaders of the Goths, took ship and sailed across the strait of the Hellespont to Asia. There they laid waste many populous cities and set fire to the renowned temple of Diana at Ephesus... Being driven from the neighbourhood of Bithynia, they destroyed Chalcedon, ... After their success, the Goths re-crossed the strait of the Hellespont, laden with booty and spoil, and returned along the same route by which they had entered the lands of Asia, sacking Troy and Ilium on the way... After the Goths had thus devastated Asia, Thrace next felt their ferocity. ...There they are said to have stayed for many days, enjoying the baths of the hot springs which are situated about twelve miles from the city of Anchiali'.

Athens was sacked, probably by a band of Heruls. The Athenian historian Dexippus urged the local inhabitants to stand up to them. Unfortunately only a few fragments of his history remain but in one surviving passage he called on small groups of Athenians to ambush the enemy and harass their retreat. Gallienus moved into Greece to oppose the invaders and he may have inflicted a defeat on the loot-ladened Heruls. He was, however, murdered in 268 to be replaced by the able Claudius II.

According to Zosimus, on Claudius' ascension, the bulk of the Goths and Heruls had joined up to lay siege to Cassandreia and Thessalonica in northern Greece. They had siege engines and were near to taking the cities when they learned that Claudius was advancing against them. Therefore they raised the sieges and retreated into the Thracian interior.

At the Battle of Naissus (Niš in modern Serbia) Claudius met and defeated the Goths and their allies. Success was attributed to the light Dalmatian cavalry on the Roman side who feigned flight to draw the Goths into pursuit so that they could be destroyed whilst in disorder. Claudius himself was an Illyrian (from modern Croatia) and the Dalmatians were his own countrymen. As the *Historia Augusta* recounts 'the valour of the Dalmatian horsemen stood out as especially great'. Claudius assumed the title 'Gothicus' after his victory but his triumph was short lived. He died in a plague which devastated the East Roman provinces in 270 and was replaced by Aurelian, who had commanded the victorious cavalry at Naissus.

The Goths were beaten but not entirely subdued after Naisus. The plague ravished their armies as well as the Romans so those who could, returned home. The prospect of loot and glory still beckoned, however. The *Historia Augusta* tells us that a band of barbarians attempted seaborne attacks on Crete and Cyprus but 'everywhere their armies were likewise stricken with pestilence and so were defeated'. In 270 another group of Goths attacked across the Danube, sacking Anchialus (Pomorie, Bulgaria) and Nicopolis (Preveza, Greece). The new emperor Aurelian launched a counter attack. He defeated the Gothic leader Cannabaudes and conducted punitive raids across the Danube. This seemed to re-establish the old frontier equilibrium. 'And so at length that most cruel of wars was brought to an end, and the Roman nation was freed from its terrors'. (*Historia Augusta*).

Chapter 3

The Calm Before the Storm

Frontiers Restored

For a century after their defeats by Claudius and Aurelian, the Goths seem to have adopted a different policy towards Rome. Enriched by the loot they had amassed during their raids, they consolidated their position to the north of the Black Sea and lower Danube to emerge as the most powerful people in the region. Rather than raiding Roman territory they found a better policy was to take payments to keep the peace, trade with the Empire and to serve in the Roman army.

Any attack against the resurgent Romans was now fraught with much greater risk than before. The opportunity presented by the chaos of the late third century had passed as under Diocletian (284-305) and Constantine (306-337) the Empire regained order and stability. The Gothic invasions of the third century had shown the Romans that it was impossible to hold every stretch of frontier against determined enemies. A new defensive strategy had evolved which aimed to deter invasion with static troops deployed along the borders (known as *limitanei*). These were backed up by regional field armies (*comitatenses*) held in central locations to plug a gap if the frontier defences were breached. Elite troops (*palatini*) were originally under the Emperor's personal command. Later, the various field armies contained both *palatini* and *comitatenses*. Constantine also disbanded the Praetorian Guard and replaced them with a new corps of guard cavalry known as the *Schola*.

Fast moving mounted reserves had proved their worth to the Romans in the war against the Goths with the Dalmatian cavalry playing a decisive role in winning the Battle of Naisus. Many more such units were created and the cavalry increased in importance and status in the early years of the fourth century although infantry still formed the backbone of all Roman armies. We have no hard evidence for a similar evolution towards cavalry amongst the Goths. It is, however, logical to assume that, as they consolidated their position in the open terrain of modern southern Ukraine, they increasingly mounted up, even if they may have preferred to fight on foot in set piece battles. Quite possibly those Gothic warriors living further east would have found fighting on horseback more advantageous that those living in the closer terrain north of the Danube.

The new Roman defensive strategy was criticised by historians from its inception. Zosimus has this to say of it:

> 'Constantine likewise adopted another measure, which gave the barbarians free access into the Roman dominions. For the Roman Empire, as I have related, was, by the care of Diocletian, protected on its remote frontiers by towns and fortresses, in which soldiers were placed. It was consequently impossible for the barbarians to pass them, there being always a sufficient force to oppose their inroads. But Constantine destroyed that security by removing the greater part of the soldiers from those barriers of the frontiers, and placing them in towns that had no need of defenders; thus depriving those who were exposed to the barbarians of all defence, and oppressing the towns that were quiet with so great a multitude of soldiers, that many of them were totally forsaken by the inhabitants. He likewise rendered his soldiers effeminate by accustoming them to public spectacles and pleasures. To speak in plain terms, he was the first cause of the affairs of the Empire declining to their present miserable state'.

The reality was that the immense borders of the Roman Empire could never be defended sufficiently strongly to become an impenetrable frontier. The many incursions of the third century demonstrated pretty clearly that Zosimus is wrong in claiming that the former frontier strategy made it impossible for the barbarians to pass. Just as the European Union today finds it impossible to seal off all access to migrants, the Romans had to accept that their borders could always be penetrated. It was better to keep concentrations of high quality forces in central locations that could deal with serious problems rather than try in vain to turn all of Europe, the Middle East and North Africa into a sealed fortress. This is not to say that the frontier was only lightly defended — far from it. In the late third and early fourth centuries Roman emperors and were very active on the Rhine and Danube and it would be a mistake to think of the field armies as passively waiting deep in the interior until they had to deal with an incursion which had bypassed or overwhelmed the *limitanei*.

The Romans had always welcomed barbarian recruits into their armies and the Goths were no exception. Several contemporary sources mention Goths serving in the Roman army in the mid fourth century. For the most part these were probably individual warriors filling out the ranks of Roman auxilia rather than Gothic units serving as allies. However, 3000 Goths are said to have joined the Romans against the Persians in 349 (Libanius); the same number are also mentioned being allied to the usurper Procopius in 365 (Ammianus Marcellinus). The *Notitia Dignitatum*, a list of offices and army units of the Roman Empire at the end of the fourth century and beginning of the fifth, lists two Gothic infantry units serving in the East. We do not know when these units, the *Visi* and *Tervingi*, came into existence. It was probably later in the fourth century but it may be that some units formed around a core of Gothic recruits were created earlier. Therefore, alongside individual recruits, there were times when fairly large numbers of Goths joined the Romans as allies in return for payments of cash and material goods paid out to clan leaders.

As the frontiers stabilized, Jordanes tells us that the Romans 'began rather to neglect the Goths'. Coincidentally with this period of neglect most of our Roman sources dry up as the Goths remained relatively quiet beyond the imperial borders. Only Jordanes continues their tale and much of what he has to say may not be entirely reliable. He asserts that Gothic warriors were frequently called on to serve in Roman armies and that they supported Constantine against Licinius (316-324). For much of the early fourth century, however, the Goths were apparently more focused on increasing their power beyond the Roman frontiers rather than intervening in Roman affairs.

Jordanes says that a Gothic leader by the name of Geberich enlarged his territory at the expense of the Asding Vandals who had moved into lands on the western fringes of the Gothic holdings north of the Danube. In a battle on the Maritsa River in the Balkans, Geberich defeated the Vandal king Visimar and the Vandal survivors were forced to seek sanctuary inside the Roman Empire to be given land to settle in Pannonia by Constantine. The battle between the Goths and Vandals may well have taken place as the two tribes had a history of near perpetual conflict. The settling of Vandal survivors in Pannonia is less likely as if that had indeed happened we might expect at least one contemporary Roman source to mention it and there is no such record.

Shortly after his victory over the Vandals, Geberich died and was succeeded by Ermanaric who continued to extend Gothic power at the expense of many neighbouring tribes including the Heruls. As the Emperor Constantine strengthened the lower Danube defences the Tervingi — the westernmost Gothic clan, started to expand westward against the Sarmatians of the middle Danube. Their success in the 330s worried the Romans enough to send an expeditionary force to intervene and halt this new Gothic expansion beyond the frontier.

Constantine strengthened the Danube frontier defences and in 328 he built a 2.5 km long bridge across the river to enable Roman armies to more easily take offensive action against the Goths to exact revenge for any raids against the Empire. Constantine then sent an army, led by his son Constantius, to devastate the Tervingi homelands. In 332, after securing hostages, the Romans concluded a formal treaty with the Tervingi in which they were paid an annual tribute and in return agreed to provide recruits for the Roman army.

The Goths Beyond the Frontier

What do we know of the Goths beyond the Danube in the first decades of the fourth century?

Jordanes' account would have us believe that at this time there was a single Gothic nation under a single ruler. This is highly unlikely. Archaeology reveals a common culture along the northwestern coast of the Black Sea extending several hundred kilometres up the Dneiper, Dniester, Prut and Danube river valleys and encompassing the Carpathian Mountains. The similarity of material goods found in this region does not necessarily mean that the Goths had supplanted all others who had previously lived in this area, nor that there was a single Gothic kingdom. In all likelihood various semi-autonomous clans inhabited the region. At times they would band together, as they did during the third century invasions, and several might acknowledge the overlordship of the same powerful leader but the political cohesion of these groups was relatively loose. Trade and treaty concessions with Rome, together with plunder from successful campaigns, allowed some of these leaders to increase their wealth and power. With this they could attract and maintain more full time warriors to serve in their households and by sharing this wealth with his followers the leader could encourage others to join him.

Roman literary sources speak of two main Gothic groups, the Tervingi to the west and the Greuthungi to the east. Traditionally these have been linked to the later Visigoths (West Goths) and Ostrogoths (East Goths) but this is anachronistic. The Visigothic kingdom in France and Spain was created by the descendants of the victors of the Battle of Adrianople, including Tervingi, Greuthungi and others. The Goths who established the Ostrogothic Kingdom of Italy in the sixth century were an amalgamation of those who had remained beyond the Roman frontier whose ties to the fourth century clans had been long broken. The Roman poet Claudian mentions 'Ostrogoths mixed with Greuthungi' in 399 so descendants of the fourth century Greuthungi ended up in both of the later Gothic kingdoms and were not synonymous with the Ostrogoths. An analysis by the modern historian Peter Heather identifies twelve different fourth century Gothic groups, five of whom contributed to the later Visigoths and Ostrogoths. None of these groups were cohesive political entities before their permanent entry into the Roman Empire. The Tervingi, being the closest to the frontier and benefiting from the material wealth that contact with Rome brought, seemed to have been less fragmented than others but they were still not yet a single nation.

Although fragmented, the various Gothic clans did rather well compared to other Germanic tribes of the time. They may not have had a permanent political structure that united all the Goths but there is no evidence that they fought amongst each other and plenty of examples to show that they could band together under a single leader to achieve their aims. Cniva may not have ruled over the Goths like a recognized medieval king but in order to defeat the Emperor Decius many different Gothic clans must have joined together under his leadership. If 3000 men did join the Romans against the Persians in the mid fourth century, various semi-independent Gothic leaders must have cooperated to provide warriors from their various holdings. Increased contact with Rome began to sow the seeds of dynastic rule. As individual leaders and their families were enriched by tribute, trade and plunder they could attract more followers and extend their influence. Other Goths saw the advantages of trading some of their independence in exchange for a share of these emerging leaders' prosperity.

When Ammianus Marcellinus describes the Greuthungi in the 370s he says that they were ruled by a king (*Latin rex*, Gothic *reiks*) and implies a rule which passed from father to son. When he speaks of the Tervingi he gives the title of 'chief magistrate' to their ruler and other sources use similar terms, usually translated as judge (*iudex*). It is not clear why these different terms were used. The later Ostrogothic kings claimed a long royal lineage going back to a legendary Gothic king called Amal and amongst whom was the Greuthungi king Ermanaric who is named by both Ammianus and Jordanes. One interpretation would be that the Greuthungi had a more autocratic structure while the Tervingi were more democratic. Yet the Tervingi were more cohesive than the Greuthungi, holding together under the pressures of the Hun migration of the 370s while the Greuthungi split apart. Another, more likely, interpretation is that the judge of the Tervingi had a sort of 'high king' status with authority over lesser kings. The Gothic word for the position was *thiudans* — the same word used by the Goths to translate the title of the East Roman Emperor.

As the Romans used different terms to describe the overlords of the Tervingi and Greuthungi confederacies it is reasonable to assume there were subtle differences even if we do not know what they were. Most probably the various clans who coalesced around the increasingly powerful leaders, would follow that leader as long as he gave them wealth and stability but would break off to go elsewhere if he failed them. In the early fourth century the Goths held together but with the arrival of the Huns this fragile cohesion fell apart.

The popular view is that the Germanic peoples were relatively democratic and self-sufficient in comparison to the oppressed masses of the autocratic Roman Empire. Much of this stems from the writings of Tacitus who wrote about the German tribes in the first century AD. Like Rousseau in the eighteenth century, Tacitus paints a portrait of the 'noble savage' compared to the degeneracy of his own society.

In the first century when Tacitus wrote about the Germans, it is probably true that their society was relatively egalitarian. Archaeological finds reveal rich burials starting to appear in the third century possibly indicating greater social stratification, especially amongst those German tribes in close contact with Rome, such as the Goths. For the most part the settlements of the Goths were unfortified villages but a number of larger fortified centres have been discovered by archeologists. A high proportion of Roman pottery alongside stone buildings indicates power centres maintained through trade, treaty or conflict with Rome.

From the third century onwards, Gothic society probably became increasingly stratified as new elites emerged through contact with Rome. Most Gothic freemen might still bear arms to defend their holdings, to join the warband of a strong leader or to take service with Rome but increasingly power shifted to a small number of men who could afford to maintain bands of professional warriors and maintain larger fortified settlements.

Christians, Pagans, Arians and Catholics

In 341 a Goth by the name of Ulfilas (Little Wolf) was consecrated Bishop at the Council of Antioch and sent north of the Danube to bring his people around to Christianity. To say he was a Goth is true but he is a good example of how ethnicity amongst the Germans was not necessarily based on race. He was descended from Roman captives taken by the Tervingi in the late third century. He grew up as a Goth, had a Gothic name and spoke Gothic as his first language but he was also fluent in Latin and Greek, and he retained his parents' Christian beliefs.

Ulfilas translated the bible into Gothic and he and his followers gradually converted his people to Christianity. This conversion did not happen overnight, nor did it go entirely smoothly. There was already a sizeable Christian community amongst the Tervingi stemming from the descendants of Roman captives, like Ulfilas himself, as well as other Romans or Roman influenced people who had been absorbed by the Goths. Initially Ulfilas' mandate was probably to minister to this community but his conversion efforts were seen by some Tervingi leaders as an attempt to spread Roman influence at their expense. This resulted in some persecutions of Christians but they were not particularly successful.

The *Passion of St Saba*, an account of the martyrdom of a Gothic Christian in 372, tells us that some of the pagan Goths refused to act against the Christians in their midst. Probably by this time many of the Gothic Tervingi had begun to convert. While some of their leaders may have viewed the spread of Christianity as weakening their power, others would have seen it as an opportunity to align more closely with Rome and maybe get preferential treatment in their dealings with the Empire.

Today we tend to think of religion as a personal matter where each individual makes up his or her own mind independently. In the fourth century this was not the case. Shared beliefs were then an important part of a people's identity. If your leaders decided that Christianity was the way of the future than you would follow suit. In post reformation Germany small principalities and even clusters of villages often switched between Catholicism and Protestantism in accordance with their leaders' decisions. The same was probably true of the Goths. If Ulfilas' priests could convince the village headman then the rest of the people would convert as well. These headmen would have converted if it suited their self-interest. Persecutions of Christians as late as 372 show that not all Tervingi would have been Christian at the time of their migration into the Roman Empire in 376. Jordanes says that conversion to Christianity was one of the conditions placed on the refugees seeking sanctuary from the Huns. Those Goths living further east probably remained mostly pagan for a while longer.

Conversion to Christianity was one issue, the version of Christianity the Goths adopted was another. Ulfilas followed the teachings of Bishop Arius (250-336) which, at the time Ulfilas went north of the Danube, were fairly widely accepted. In simple layman's terms Arius believed that Jesus was a man created by God the Father. He was from God but Jesus and the Father were not the same being. Others held that the Trinity of the Father, Son and Holy Ghost were one and the same with no differentiation or hierarchy between them. This is necessarily a very simplistic interpretation. The subtle nuances surrounding the nature of the Trinity resulted in the deaths of thousands of believers on both sides as the various adherents of one idea or the other persecuted their opponents with fanatical fervour. The Council of Nicaea in 325 attempted to draw a line under the controversy, defining the relationship of the Son and Father as 'of the same substance'. As a result the idea that the Father, Son and Holy Ghost were the same being became known as the Nicene belief and from this we get the Nicene Creed which is today the official doctrine of the Catholic Church.

The Nicaean Council did not settle the matter. Furious, frequently deadly debates, continued as the Roman Empire became consumed with the relationship between Jesus and God. At a second Ecumenical Council at Constantinople in 381 the Arian version that the Son and Father were similar but not the same, was finally declared heretical and the Nicene Creed became the only acceptable interpretation of Christianity for Romans. By this time, however, the Goths and most other Germanic people had adopted Arius' interpretation. In the mid fourth century most Romans were Christians and many Goths were pagans. Half a century later the two people were still divided by religion with Romans Catholic Nicaean Christians while the Goths were Arians.

Renewed Conflict

For most of the first half of the fourth century, Goths and Romans enjoyed a period of relative peace and stability. Beyond the Danube, the Goths benefited from trade with Rome and secured their position at the expense of their neighbours. The Romans once again had a reasonably secure frontier and benefited from Gothic recruits and allies in their wars against the Persians and various usurpers.

In 365 Procopius, a military tribune who had served the Emperor Julian, made a bid for power and rose against Valens the new ruler of the eastern half of the Roman Empire. He won over the legions of Thrace to his cause and also secured the aid of 3000 Goths. Valens was victorious, Procopius was killed and then Valens set about punishing the Goths for having supported Procopius against him.

> 'Victor, the Master of Horse (*Magister Equitum*), was sent to the Goths to inquire, without disguise, why a nation friendly to the Romans, and bound to it by treaties of equitable peace, had given the support of its arms to a man who was waging war against their lawful emperor. And they, to excuse their conduct by a valid defence, produced the letters from the above-mentioned Procopius, in which he alleged that he had assumed the sovereignty as his due, as the nearest relation to Constantine's family; and they asserted that this was a fair excuse for their error'. (Ammianus Marcellinus)

This passage is indicative of the relations between the Goths and Romans since the end of the third century. In the Roman view, the Goths may have been beyond the formal frontier but they expected them to act almost as a client state. The reported Gothic response is equally indicative of their awareness of Roman politics and their subservience to the greater power beyond the Danube. Just as today a small state cannot ignore the wishes of the USA, EU, Russia or China without suffering the consequences, so it was for the Goths. Valens was not impressed by the Gothic response and so he assembled an army to punish them. Making a bridge of boats he crossed the Danube.

> 'He [Valens] traversed the country in every direction. He met with no enemy to be either defeated or even alarmed by his advance; they having all been so terrified at the approach of so formidable a host, that they had fled to the high mountains of the Serri, [Carpathians] which were inaccessible to all except those who knew the country... Therefore, that he [Valens] might not waste the whole summer, and return without having effected anything, he sent forward Arinthaeus, the Master of Foot, with some light forces, who seized on a portion of their [Gothic] families, which were overtaken as they were wandering over the plains before coming to the steep and winding defiles of the mountains. And having obtained this advantage, which chance put in his way, he returned with

his men without having suffered any loss, and indeed without having inflicted any'. (Ammianus Marcellinus)

The following year Valens again attempted a punitive expedition against the Goths but his efforts were hampered by floods on the Danube. Valens' desultory campaign went on for three years. He managed to bring about some sort of engagement with the Greuthungi and 'after some trivial skirmishes, he defeated Athanaric, at that time the most powerful man of the tribe, who dared to resist him with what he fancied an adequate force, but was compelled to flee for his life'.

Valens' campaigns produced no great victories. Like the Russians facing Napoleon and Hitler, the Goths simply melted away when confronted by the overwhelming force of the Imperial army. However the Roman incursions disrupted the trade upon which the Goths had become dependent. Therefore, although undefeated in battle, the Gothic leaders made overtures for peace. The situation the Goths found themselves in was typical of most barbarian tribes on the Roman frontier for centuries. A punitive expedition penetrating their heartlands upset the balance. Even if the Romans could not bring them to battle their economy had become so dependent on Rome that a lengthy disruption to the status quo could not be endured. After three years of tough campaigning beyond the frontiers, Valens too was no doubt anxious to settle the issue and return to deal with the internal politics of the Empire. All he needed was to be able to portray his campaign as a victory.

So a peace treaty was concluded between Valens and Athanaric. According to Ammianus Marcellinus, Athanaric was bound by an oath to his father to never set foot on Roman territory. Therefore the treaty was concluded on boats in the middle of the Danube where Valens and Athanaric met to conclude peace terms.

'When this had been arranged, and hostages had been given, Valens returned to Constantinople, whither afterwards Athanaric fled, when he was driven from his native land by a faction among his kinsmen; and he died in that city, and was buried with splendid ceremony according to the Roman fashion'. (Ammianus Marcellinus)

This passage sheds some insight into the political climate amongst the Goths. A Gothic king was expected to bring victory and material wealth to his followers. Athanaric had not been defeated by Valens but, although we do not know the terms of the peace treaty, many Goths must have seen it as a capitulation. No doubt Athanaric received gifts from Valens on signing the treaty but many of the other Gothic leaders whose lands had been devastated by the Roman campaign may have felt that they had not been adequately compensated. Athanaric's reputation amongst his people seems to have been weakened and later when the Huns invaded many of the Goths deserted him.

Interestingly, Ammianus first says that Valens fought the Gruethungi, implying that Athanaric was their leader. When he describes the Hun invasion a few years later he states that Athanaric was the Judge of the Tervingi. Quite possibly the Romans would not have been entirely clear on the differences between the various Gothic peoples nor the allegiances of the various bands they fought. They had managed to bring a Gothic leader to the treaty table and as far as they were concerned that was it. That Athanaric may not have had the support of all the Goths was his problem, not theirs.

Chapter 4

The Great Migration

The Refugees

In the 370s the fragile equilibrium between the Goths and Romans was shattered by the arrival of the Huns on the eastern fringes of the Gothic territories. These central Asian nomads, first overran the Alans — another nomadic people living on the eastern fringes of Gothic lands to the north of the Black Sea. According to Ammianus Marcellinus, the Huns then linked up with the surviving Alans and pushed westward into the lands held by the Gruethungi.

> 'And when they [Huns and Alans] had united them to themselves, with increased boldness they made a sudden incursion into the extensive and fertile districts of Ermanaric [King of the Gruethungi], a very warlike prince, and one whose numerous gallant actions of every kind had rendered him formidable to all the neighbouring nations'.

Ermanaric was overwhelmed and if Ammianus is to be believed, committed suicide to be replaced by Vithimiris. A slightly different version of the story is told by Jordanes who attributes Ermanaric's death to a revenge attack taken by two brothers from a subject tribe. Their sister, Sunilda was torn apart by wild horses on Ermanaric's orders to avenge some treachery by her husband who had seen the Hun invasion as an opportunity to break away from the King's authority. According to Jordanes' tale Ermanaric was gravely wounded in the attack and died shortly afterwards. Jordanes also tells of a dispute amongst the Goths which resulted in the division between Visigoths and Ostrogoths. As we have already seen these names are anachronistic but it is highly likely that serious divisions would have resulted from the intense pressures the Goths were now under. The authority of the Gothic leaders was already weakened by Valens' campaign and this new pressure from the Huns would have stretched their followers' loyalty even further.

The popular image is of an unrelenting onslaught of Huns who suddenly sprung up from the depths of Central Asia to sweep all before them. Yet it was probably much more gradual as the centre of Hun power remained well to the east long after the Battle of Adrianople. Ammianus tells us that the initial threat to the

Gruethungi was from displaced Alans rather than Huns and that Vithimitis actually employed some Hun mercenaries to help fend them off.

> 'He [Vithimiris] for some time maintained a resistance to the Alans, relying on the aid of other tribes of the Huns, whom by large promises of pay he had won over to his party; but, after having suffered many losses, he was defeated by superior numbers and slain in battle. He left an infant son named Viderichus, of whom Alatheus and Saphrax undertook the guardianship, both generals of great experience and proved courage. And when they, yielding to the difficulties of the crisis, had given up all hope of being able to make an effectual resistance, they retired with caution till they came to the river Dniester, which lies between the Danube and the Dnieper, and flows through a vast extent of country'.

The immediate effect of the Hun expansion westward seems to have been to break the fragile political leadership of the Goths and undermine their position as the most powerful people north of the Black Sea and lower Danube. For years the Goths had been consolidating their strength at the expense of their neighbours. Now, weakened by Valens and attacked by new enemies, the fragility of their position became apparent.

The Tervingi too began to feel the pressure. Alatheus and Saphrax fled westward with some Greuthungi while other eastern Goths no doubt made accommodation with the Huns and adapted to the changing circumstances. Athanaric, who still led the Tervingi, made defensive preparations and attempted to hold the Dniester against any incursions. The Huns, however, bypassed Athanaric's defences, crossed the river at night and took the Goths by surprise. Suffering heavy casualties, Athanaric withdrew and began to fortify a new defensive line between the Pruth and Danube rivers, probably adapting old Roman fortifications.

The Huns did not let up. As Ammianus recounts, while the defensive works were going on 'the Huns kept pressing on his [Athanaric's] traces with great speed'. In the end Athanaric was undone not by a defeat in battle but rather by internal dissension. Athanaric's position had already been weakened by his treaty with Valens. The disruption caused by the Huns began to result in deprivation or maybe even famine amongst the Goths. New leaders emerged as many Goths sought other solutions. 'And then the greater part of the population which, because of their want of necessaries had deserted Athanaric, resolved to flee and to seek a home remote from all knowledge of the barbarians'. (Ammianus Marcellinus)

This large group of deserters, led by Alavivus and Fritigern, decided that their best recourse was to seek refuge inside the Roman Empire. They sent ambassadors to Valens asking him for sanctuary in return for providing troops for his army. This seemed like a good deal to Valens. At a stroke he would have a large body of new and able recruits at no cost to his treasury. This would help stabilize the Danube frontier allowing him to concentrate his forces against Persia. He could not have foreseen the flood gates he was about to open. Ammianus Marcellinus takes up the story:

> 'Full of this hope he [Valens] sent forth several officers to bring this ferocious people [the Tervingi] and their wagons into our territory. And such great pains were taken to gratify this nation which was destined to overthrow the Empire of Rome that not one was left behind, not even of those who were stricken with mortal disease. Moreover, having obtained permission of the Emperor to cross the Danube and to cultivate some districts in Thrace, they crossed the stream day and night, without ceasing, embarking in troops on board ships and rafts, and canoes made of the hollow trunks of trees, as the Danube is the most difficult of all rivers to navigate. It was at that time swollen with continual rains, and a great many were drowned, who, because they were too numerous for the vessels, tried to swim across, and in spite of all their exertions were swept away by the stream.
> 'In this way, through the turbulent zeal of violent people, the ruin of the Roman empire was brought on. The unhappy officers who were entrusted with the charge of conducting the multitude of the barbarians across the river, though they repeatedly endeavoured to calculate their numbers, at last abandoned the attempt as hopeless'.

As the European Union has learned in recent times, dealing with a mass influx of refugees is incredibly difficult even for the most competent of officials. Unfortunately the senior Roman officers in charge of the region (Lupicinus and Maximus) were not up to the task. Ammianus claims that 'their sinister greed was the source of all our troubles… they displayed the greatest profligacy in their injurious treatment of the foreigners dwelling in our territory, against whom no crime could be alleged'.

Apparently the Roman border officials made a handsome profit out of feeding the starving refugees. According to Ammianus, although the Tervingi were supposed to have been moved on from the border to be re-settled further south, Roman officials kept them in a refugee camp on the Danube because they were making such a good profit by selling them poor quality food at inflated prices. Another explanation for keeping the refugees cooped up on the border could be put down to panic when the sheer numbers overwhelmed all expectations. The situation facing the Romans in 376 would have been very similar to that facing many European nations in more or less the same part of the world in 2015/16. They had expected and were prepared for a number of refugees but nothing like the numbers they were suddenly faced with.

While the Tervingi were struggling to survive on the Roman side of the Danube, Alatheus and Saphrax's Greuthungi and Alans had moved up to the opposite bank, joined by another band led by Farnobius. These new arrivals also requested asylum but it was refused and the Romans attempted to close the border.

The Greuthungi were not prepared to take no for an answer. When Lupicinus' troops were distracted, dealing with some trouble amongst the Tervingi, they made their move.

> 'Seeing that our men were engaged elsewhere, and that the boats which patrolled the river to prevent their crossing had ceased to operate, the Greuthungi took advantage of the opportunity to slip over on roughly made rafts and pitched their camp a long way from Fritigern. The latter, however, whose native shrewdness served to protect him against any eventuality, found a way to both obey his [Valens'] orders and at the same time unite with these powerful kings [Alatheus, Saphrax and Farnobius]'. (Ammianus Marcellinus).

Although they had made it over the Danube the Goths were still without permanent homes and were desperately short of food. With the new arrivals, increased numbers would have made it nearly impossible to find any food in the over-foraged areas of the river crossing. Although not yet in open revolt, the Goths took matters into their own hands. In defiance of the local authorities the Tervingi broke out of their containment area on the Danube to strike south for the fertile regions around Marcianople (modern Devnja, Bulgaria).

The Battle of Marcianople

The stage was set for conflict and it would only take a spark to set it off. That spark was a bungled assassination attempt on the Gothic leaders as Lupicinus attempted to bring them back under control. He invited Alavivus and Fritigern to a sumptuous dinner party in Marcianople, letting them believe that they would discuss provisions for their starving people. Lupicinus only allowed the leaders and their immediate bodyguards to enter the town and then kept the others outside his headquarters while the leaders dined.

Lupicinus ordered his men to kill the Gothic bodyguards while others were to man the walls to prevent any rescue attempt. Ammianus' description of the incident is confusing but clearly things went awry. Fighting broke out and some Goths outside 'killed and stripped of their arms a large contingent of troops and laid siege to the town'. It is not clear whether Lupicinus intended to keep the leaders hostage or kill them but Alavivus apparently perished while Fritigern managed to escape. Jordanes says that Fritigern managed to fight his way out while Ammianus says that he was able to convince Lupicinus that he would try to pacify his followers to avoid battle.

However he managed it, Fritigern rejoined his people and together they began looting the farms and villas surrounding Marcianople. Lupicinus marshalled his troops and marched out of the town to challenge them. A battle was fought nine miles from the city, most likely to the west. It is unclear how many troops were involved. The Goths were probably only Fritigern's Tervingi as there is no mention of Alatheus, Saphrax or Farnobius at the dinner. At Adrianople two years later the Tervingi probably had around 10,000 warriors. At this point Fritigern probably had fewer followers than that.

The full strength of the Roman border army along the lower Danube was around 20–30,000 *limitanei*. These were relatively static border forces and given the tremendous instability and danger along the Danube it is unlikely that Lupicinus would have withdrawn any of them back to Marcianople. According to the *Notitia Dignitatum*, the Roman field army in Thrace at the end of the fourth century had seven *vexillationes* of cavalry (3500 troopers at full strength) and twenty-one legions (20–30,000 infantry at full strength). Although many of these units were raised after 378 it does give us some indication of the total forces available to Lupicinus. It is unlikely, however, that he would have had all of them with him at Marcianople. The Tervingi leaders would not have accepted an invitation to dinner with the full Roman field army in attendance and many troops would have been keeping an eye on the Gruethungi. Others were probably stationed at central locations ready to reinforce the increasingly porous frontier. Ammianus makes the point that Lupicinus mustered his troops with 'tumultuous speed' and advanced with 'more haste than caution', implying that he did not take time to call in more troops from further afield before engaging the Goths. No doubt, after bungling the assassination attempt he wanted to rectify the situation as quickly as possible.

Therefore, the two armies that met outside Marcianople in 376 probably numbered less than 10,000 men each. The Goths were ill-fed desperate refugees who had managed to procure arms and equipment from the Romans they engaged and defeated earlier outside the city walls. We can only assume that as Lupicinus' troops formed up to meet them they were as confident as any body of trained troops could be going out to deal with what they saw as a barbarian rabble.

The Romans deployed defensively and waited for the Gothic charge. Probably most, maybe all, of the troops on both sides were on foot. Ammianus describes what happened next. 'The barbarians hurled themselves recklessly on our lines, dashing their shield upon the bodies of their opponents and running them through with spears and swords. In this furious and bloody assault our standards were snatched from us and our tribunes and the greater part of our men perished, all but their luckless commander. While the others were fighting his one aim was to get away, and he made for the city at a gallop. After this the enemy [the Goths] armed themselves with Roman weapons and roamed at large unresisted'.

The situation for the Tervingi had now changed dramatically. No longer a desperate band of refugees barely able to secure the necessities of life, they had defeated a Roman army, had equipped themselves with Roman food, arms and armour, and now suddenly found themselves as the masters of Thrace. The remaining detachments of the Thracian field army would have remained bottled up in the key cities, none of them individually strong enough to take on the now well-equipped Goths. Valens, with the main East Roman army, was far to the east facing the Persians while the West Roman Emperor Gratian was busy along the Rhine frontier.

Things began to look up further when Roman troops of Gothic origin joined in the revolt. These men, led by Sueridus and Colias were in winter quarters at Adrianople (modern Erdine in Turkey). When they were ordered to the east out of fear that they would join up with Fritigern's Tervingi, they did just that. In panic the chief magistrate of Adrianople called out the mob to attack the Gothic troops. Like modern police facing rioters 'the Goths remained immovable but when they were finally driven desperate by curses and abuse and a few missiles hurled at them, they broke out into open rebellion' (Ammianus Marcellinus). The Gothic Roman troops turned on the mob, dispersed them and then joined forces with Fritigern.

Fritigern's army was further swelled by Gothic slaves held by the Romans, Roman prisoners who decided to switch sides, and Roman slaves who saw the Goths as a better alternative to their current masters. Amongst the latter were a large number of miners from the gold mines of the Thracian and Macedonian mountains. Ammianus says that these men were particularly useful to the Goths as they could direct them to 'concealed stores of grain and hidden corners where people had taken refuge'.

Ad Salices and the Campaign of 377

Throughout the winter of 376/7 Fritigern would have been able to sustain his forces from the towns and villas he had plundered. His situation was far better than it had been in the refugee camps on the Danube but he had no reliable source of food or supplies to maintain his growing number of followers. He had defeated a Roman army in battle and there was not yet any other Roman force in the region which could stand up to him. However, his only hope for long term survival was to force the Romans to conclude a peace and give him and his followers land to settle and farm — in effect re-affirming the original terms the Tervingi had been given by Valens when they crossed the Danube. The longer it took to achieve this the greater the chances of being forced into submission by starvation.

With no supply source the Goths had to forage in small bands over a very wide area. This meant that bands could be picked off and destroyed if the Romans were able to concentrate their better equipped forces against them. Fritigern's problem was that he needed large enough numbers of men to defeat the Roman field army and hopefully force favourable peace terms but the more men he gathered in any one place increased the chances that hunger would defeat him. Furthermore, having no home base the Gothic warriors were hampered by large numbers of non-combatants who needed food and protection.

Although a protracted campaign of attrition favoured the Romans, Valens could not simply stand back and allow the Goths free reign in Thrace without losing political support. Therefore he sent Victor, his *Magister Equitum* (master of horse), to conclude a peace with Persia so he could withdraw troops from Armenia. These he sent west to engage the Goths in a guerrilla campaign under the command of Profuturus and Trajan. He also called on his co-Emperor Gratian to send help from the west. Ammianus tells us that the Armenian legions had a good record in conventional battle but they were not used to this sort of irregular warfare. Nonetheless they managed to drive some Gothic bands out of the lowlands and forced them to take refuge in the Balkan mountains where it was hoped they would 'ultimately perish from hunger'.

Meanwhile Gratian responded to his uncle's request for aid by sending the age-ing general Frigeridus with 'Pannonian and Transalpine auxiliaries'. He also dispatched Richomeres, his commander of household troops (*Comes Domesticorum*) with a number of units drawn from the Gallic field army. When these troops were ordered to the East there were mass desertions apparently encouraged by Merobaudes, the *Magister Peditum* of the West who did not want Gaul stripped of her defences since he feared it would leave the province open to raids from across the Rhine. This was a justifiable fear as later events were to prove.

It is not clear where all the Goths were as the Roman armies closed on them from East and West. Some were blocked up in the Balkan mountains, some probably at large in Thrace, while others were in the low-lying regions near the mouth of the Danube. It is probable that the latter were newcomers, possibly Greuthungi, who had recently crossed the river. It was this group that the Roman reinforcements converged on (see Map 3).

Frigeridus and Richomeres linked up with Profuturus and Trajan at *Ad Salices* (by the willows) in the Dobrogei region of modern Romania. 'Not far away was a countless horde of barbarians who had drawn up their wagons in a circle inside which they were taking their ease and enjoying their rich plunder as if they were protected by city walls'. (Ammianus Marcellinus)

Richomeres took command of the combined Roman forces and looked for an opportunity to attack. The Romans were not strong enough to assault the Gothic wagon laager so they waited, knowing that the Goths would eventually have to move to find food or to avoid disease from a fouled camp. Once they moved the Romans could fall on the vulnerable column and wear it down with a series of hit and run attacks. The Goths were informed of the Roman intentions by deserters and so they remained in place and sent out messengers to call in the scattered bands foraging close by.

A large party of reinforcements reached the Gothic camp one evening and there was a clamour amongst the warriors in the wagon laager to attack at once despite the approach of nightfall. The Gothic leaders (Fritigern was apparently not with this band) managed to hold their men back but both Romans and Goths spent a sleepless night in the knowledge that battle was approaching.

Early the next morning the Goths attacked. We have no idea of the numbers of troops involved in the battle but they were clearly not large. The Roman forces consisted of the Armenian legions, Frigeridus' auxiliaries and Richomeres' depleted Gallic units. It is possible that not all the Armenians were present since some may have been detached to watch the Balkan passes, although this may have been delegated to the remnants of the Thracian field army or even local *limitanei*. A reasonable estimate of the Roman forces would have been in the region of 5-6,000 men — almost all infantry although there was a small body of cavalry. Ammianus says that the Goths had more troops and since they were tempted to attack this could well be true. There is no mention of any of the Gothic leaders present so, although this was a significant band, it was not the main Gothic force and it must have been smaller than the 10,000 Tervingi following Fritigern. Like the Romans, most of the Goths fought on foot and some may have managed to equip themselves with Roman weapons and armour. Their army also included a number of Roman deserters.

The Goths left the wagon laager and seized some high ground from which to charge down onto the Roman line which was forming up close by. Ammianus provides a colourful account of what happened next:

'The armies on both sides advanced cautiously then halted and stood immovable, the warriors, with mutual sternness, surveying each other with fierce looks. The Romans in every part of their line sang warlike songs, with a voice rising from a lower to a higher key, which they call *barritus* ... light skirmishes began as each army began to assail the other with javelins and other similar missiles. Then with threatening shouts they rushed in to close combat, and packing their shields together, they came foot to foot with their foes. The barbarians... broke our left wing; but as it recoiled, it fell back on a strong body of reserves which was vigorously brought up on their flank, and supported them just as they were on the very point of destruction...The cavalry, too, pressed on, cutting down all who fled with terrible and mighty wounds on their backs; as also on both sides did the infantry, slaughtering and hamstringing those who had fallen down, and through fear were unable to fly'.

The battle went on all day and as evening came on both sides withdrew exhausted to their respective camps. Ammianus tries to put a positive spin on the outcome by claiming fewer losses but while the Romans may not have been routed it was certainly a strategic defeat. The only Roman army in the region able to take offensive action against the Goths was now no longer a viable fighting force. The Goths who had fought at Ad Salices were still on the Roman side of the Danube and they were not the only ones.

Apart from its strategic significance, the Battle of Ad Salices gives us a rare insight into the fighting methods of both Goths and Romans of the time. Most contemporary battle accounts are brief one-liners leaving us to imagine the details. Others are so highly stylized as to be nearly useless in working out how the armies actually fought. Ammianus Marcellinus was not only a historian, he was also an army officer who had experienced battle himself. Although he often falls back on stereotypical depictions of wild barbarians against steady Romans, his account of Ad Salices is both detailed and reasonably balanced.

We see how the Romans deployed defensively in two lines, or possibly with a main line and significant reserve. The Gothic attack was not a wild, disorganized, mad rush. Instead they first seized the high ground then they advanced cautiously and deliberately, halting at javelin range. Then the two lines tried to intimidate each other and raise their own morale by shouting war cries, banging on their shields and insulting their opponents. This gives way to light skirmishing and an exchange of missiles at close range. This is mostly javelins thrown from the front ranks but probably also archers shooting from rear ranks over the heads of the spearmen. Ammianus also mentions slings being used. Finally the two shieldwalls crash together, each trying to force the other back in a massive shoving match. In this case the Roman left wing gave way but reserves from the second line restored the situation. Cavalry, still a minority in both armies, hovered on the flanks, seeking opportunities and pursuing fugitives.

After Ad Salices the Romans withdrew back to Marcianople and made no further attempt to engage the Goths in battle. Instead they positioned troops to block all the passes leading south from the Balkans while the various Gothic bands apparently took no further offensive action against the Romans. 'So our soldiers, seizing the opportunity, raised barriers to shut the other hordes of barbarians among the defiles of the Balkans, in hope that this destructive host being thus hemmed in between the Danube and the wilderness, and having no road by which to escape, must perish by famine, since everything which could serve to sustain life had been conveyed into the fortified cities, and these cities were safe from any attempt of the barbarians to besiege them, since they were wholly ignorant of the use of warlike engines'. (Ammianus Marcellinus)

Valens appointed Saturninus to take over command from Trajan and Profuturus, Richomeres was recalled to Gaul, while Frigeridus moved south to Beroea (modern Stara Zagora, Bulgaria) where he fortified a position that watched the key passes from Illyricum in the west and the central Balkans to the north. Ammianus says that Saturninus arranged a system of outposts and pickets which managed to keep the Goths bottled up in the inhospitable regions. Although the Goths made several attempts to break out they were driven back each time. Hemmed into mountain defiles or along the bank of the Danube they could not join forces to overwhelm the Roman blockade. If large numbers did manage to congregate they would suffer the prospect of starvation due to lack of forage and supplies.

One band of Goths, probably the same group that had fought at Ad Salices, made an alliance with some Huns and Alans and enticed them across the Danube. It must have been a fairly significant number of Huns and Alans who came across since they altered the balance enough that Saturninus felt it necessary to concentrate his forces to avoid individual outposts being overrun. This allowed the Goths, Huns and Alans to break out into the lowlands of southern Thrace and range over the countryside in search of supplies.

Frigeridus' West Roman troops in their fortified position at Beroea were now in danger of being caught between Fritigern's Tervingi and this new group of Goths, Huns and Alans which had broken through Saturninus' lines. Frigeridus therefore withdrew westward over the Succi pass back to Illyricum. On the way he encountered Farnobius' band of Greuthungi, which had been reinforced by some Taifali (another eastern Germanic tribe). Farnobius was killed in the battle that followed, his warriors surrendered and were shipped off to work the farms of northern Italy.

The Road to Adrianople

Apart from Farnobius' defeat in the mountain passes, the Goths so far had the better of the Romans in every engagement. A ragged band of refugees had been able to equip themselves from the battlefield and the armouries of Marcianople. They had been reinforced by the Gothic-Roman troops from Adrianople as well as Roman deserters, escaped slaves and others who saw greater opportunity with the Goths than with the Roman authorities who so far had failed to protect them. New arrivals took advantage of the chaos created by Fritigern's band to cross the Danube along with Huns, Alans, Taifali and no doubt others as well. Having broken free of Saturninus' blockade they were able to feed themselves from the countryside.

The typical pattern of barbarian incursions was initial success, followed by a Roman counter-attack which would inevitably destroy the invaders. Then there would be a punitive expedition which would restore the status quo with new more pliable barbarian leaders emerging to replace those who had been defeated. This was what happened in the Marcomannic wars and in the Gothic wars of the third century.

In early 378 this was probably what most people would have expected to happen yet again. Despite their successes in the field, the Gothic position was still pretty tenuous. Forced to split up into relatively small groups to make foraging possible, they knew that before long they would face a major Roman counter-attack. In former times they might return to their homes across the Danube taking their slaves and loot with them. Unfortunately their homeland no longer existed.

We do not know how many separate bands there were. Most of them were apparently centred on the river valleys south of the Balkan mountains around the towns of Dibaltum, Cabyle and Beroea in modern Bulgaria. Other bands were still north of the Balkans in the Danube valley since Ammianus mentions a fortified Gothic position at Nicopolis ad Istrum which is 90 kms due north of Beroea on the other side of the mountains (see Map 3).

A counter-attack was exactly what Valens was planning but he had problems. Learning that Gratian was sending troops to the East to help his uncle, the Lentienses (an Alamannic tribe) decided to take advantage of the weakened Rhine frontier to launch a series of raids, followed up by a major incursion. This not only tied up Gratian but also forced him to recall some troops that were on their way to the East. Although Valens had managed to patch up an uneasy peace with Persia he could not afford to withdraw all his best troops from the Persian frontier to deal with the Goths. In the spring of 378 he personally moved from Antioch (his headquarters for operations against Persia) to Constantinople. There he had to deal with an outbreak of popular discontent. This was partly a result of the largely Catholic population objecting to Valens' Arian faith, no doubt aggravated by the proximity of the Arian Goths and the dismal Roman campaign so far.

Needing to buy more time, Valens appointed the western general Sebastian as *Magister Militum* to replace Trajan. Taking a picked body of troops, by selecting 300 men from various units, Sebastian waged a guerrilla war against the various Gothic bands to give Valens more time to marshal his forces. According to Zosimus, Sebastian's force was 2000 men strong — a reasonable number for conducting special operations where quality and experience were more important than quantity.

An indication of the kind of campaign being fought out in Thrace in the early months of 378 is provided by Ammianus when he describes an action in which

Sebastian engaged a group of Goths to the northwest of Adrianople. 'Towards evening he [Sebastian] caught sight of some Gothic raiding parties near the Maritsa River. He concealed himself for a while behind dikes and bushes and then crept forward quietly under cover of night to attack them in their sleep. His success was so complete that all perished except for a few who saved themselves by speed of foot'.

Sebastian's guerrilla campaign began to have some effect. Fritigern and the other Gothic leaders realised that they were in danger of being defeated piecemeal while their bands were split up foraging and looting. Valens was concentrating the East Roman Army at Melanthias, about 20 kms from Constantinople. Gratian meanwhile, having defeated the Lentienses, was proceeding eastwards with a small body of troops whom Ammianus Marcellinus describes as 'lightly armed'.

Realising that the showdown was coming, Fritigern decided to act first rather than be caught passively in a pincer movement from east and west. He recalled his followers and allies to the vicinity of Cabyle 'and then quickly evacuated the area, intending to keep his people in open country where they could not be surprised or suffer from lack of food'. (Ammianus Marcellinus)

As Gratian approached from the west, Valens moved westward towards Adrianople. His intention was probably to continue on from Adrianople, along the Maritsa River towards Philippopolis and then move north where he hoped to trap the Goths between his army and Gratian's coming down from the Danube. Unfortunately for Valens, Fritigern moved first, striking directly south from Cabyle, following the Tundzha River towards Nike, a way station 15 kms east of Adrianople, where he hoped to cut the Roman supply lines. Ammianus tells us that Valens sent a body of archers and a troop of horse to block the Goths but this seems like a rather inadequate force for such a big job. Perhaps at this stage Valens did not yet realise that Fritigern had marshalled his forces and was approaching in strength.

Ammianus' account leads us to believe that Valens was already west of Adrianople when he learned that a large Gothic army was moving south along the Tundzha to cut him off. Once he realised that this was more than a small group of raiders he returned to Adrianople to consider his options. Should he attack at once or should he wait for Gratian to join him?

Valens' scouts reported that Fritigern had 10,000 men. We do not know for certain how many troops Valens had but it must have been at least 15,000 men and quite possibly more. If he thought he outnumbered the Goths it would have been very tempting for Valens to offer battle without waiting for the western reinforcements. After two years of Gothic depredations in Thrace, his political standing was now at a fairly low ebb in Constantinople and if he failed to act he would not only risk his supply lines being cut but the restless populace would feel even more abandoned by their Emperor. It was situations like this that tended to encourage the rise of usurpers.

Fritigern's Goths moved quite slowly over the next three days. Encumbered by wagons and non-combatants it would have been difficult going over the rough, hilly terrain from Cabyle towards Adrianople. The ground only opens up about 20 kms north of Adrianople when the Goths would have been able to move more easily. Fritigern's Tervingi was not the only band of Goths on the move. Answering his call to join forces the Greuthungi and Alans under Alatheus and Saphrax were also converging on Adrianople. While Fritigern probably followed the east bank of the Tundzha, it may be that Alatheus and Saphrax followed up behind along the west bank, approaching the rendezvous by a different route. If the Greuthungi and Alans were on a different route it may account for the fact that Valens' scouts underestimated the size of the whole Gothic force.

The Gothic Army

At this point we should consider the size, composition and fighting methods of the Gothic army which fought at Adrianople. We know that Valens' scouts reported that they were 10,000 strong but we also know that they had underestimated the Gothic strength but unfortunately we do not know how far off they were in their estimate. Numbers as high as 200,000 men are quoted in some accounts but even the most incompetent of scouts could not mistake 200,000 men for 10,000. It is most likely that the Roman scouts only noticed Fritigern's force but had missed the other contingents which were converging on Adrianople from other directions and along other routes. Alatheus, Saphrax and the victors at Ad Salices probably commanded at least as many men as Fritigern. If this was the case then a number closer to 20,000 seems likely for the whole force.

The Gothic army was not a single cohesive force. They were a people on the move and their ranks were filled with migrants, Roman deserters and opportunists from other tribes. Every able-bodied male would have fought with whatever weapons he had been able to get his hands on. Most of these would have come from Roman armouries or previous battlefields although newer arrivals may have brought their native equipment across the Danube. The men of fighting age were accompanied by a much larger number of non-combatants — women, children, old men and slaves.

The Gothic ranks were filled by men of many different origins. We know that Fritigern's Tervingi had been augmented by the Romano-Gothic units commanded by Sueridus and Colias and that they had also picked up other Roman deserters and escaped slaves. Alatheus and Saphrax commanded a core of Greuthungi but Saphrax himself was probably an Alan and no doubt had a number of Alan

followers. We have already seen that the victors at Ad Salices also included contingents of Huns and Alans in addition to Goths and that some Taifali joined up
with Farnobius. Although the latter group had been defeated it does show that an
unknown number of other non-Gothic tribes had taken the opportunity presented
by the collapse of the Danube defences to join in.

The Tervingi had been at least partially disarmed when they initially crossed the
Danube in 376 but had been able to equip themselves from the Roman armouries
at Marcianople. It is quite likely that they had also been able to round up a good
number of horses from the countryside but much like their third century ancestors
they probably still preferred to dismount to fight on foot.

Many historians think that the Greuthungi may have been more inclined to
mounted combat than their Tervingi cousins. This is based on two facts. Firstly
that their homeland was further east, in the open terrain of modern southern
Ukraine where it would be natural to build up a good horse herd. Secondly that
Alatheus and Saphrax's contingent fought on horseback at Adrianople while
Fritigern's Tervingi fought on foot.

Although there may be some truth to this, it would be wrong to assume that
the Gruethungi were primarily mounted warriors while the Tervingi were primarily infantrymen. It is unlikely that many horses could have been ferried across
the Danube and any that did probably ended up as food in the early days when
the Goths were facing starvation. After the conflict broke out both Tervingi and
Greuthungi would have rounded up horses and as many men as possible would
have mounted up for strategic mobility. If the Greuthungi had maintained good
chargers back in their homelands, the nags they managed to capture would not have
been of the same calibre and there would have been little opportunity to train horse
and rider together to make a true heavy cavalry team. As we will see, the fact that
the Greuthungi fought mounted at Adrianople while the Tervingi were on foot was
a result of circumstance rather than a tactical division between cavalry and infantry.

While most Gothic warriors fought hand to hand with spear and shield, we have
already seen that they made good use of missile weapons including both javelins
and arrows. In the fifth century, Flavius Vegetius claimed that Roman troops had
begun to abandon armour and 'in consequence of this our troops in their engagements with the Goths were often 'overwhelmed by showers of arrows'. Much of
what Vegetius writes needs to be taken with a grain of salt but it is interesting that
he singles out Gothic archery. Given what we know of their victory over Decius
in the third century it is reasonable to assume that while the more experienced
warriors formed the front ranks of a shieldwall they were supported by a number
of archers and javelinmen launching missiles over their heads or from the flanks.
This is how the Romans fought and it is likely that the Goths adopted similar
tactics.

The Huns and Alans, on the other hand, were exclusively mounted warriors. Ammianus says of the Huns that they were 'ill-fitted to fight on foot and remained glued to their horses', adding that the Alans were similar. On the assumption that most of the Huns and Alans were relatively recent arrivals, called in to support the victors at Ad Salices, it is probable that they had not experienced the same deprivations as the Goths who had crossed earlier. Therefore they may have been able to bring many of their good mounts across the Danube, replacing casualties with newly captured horses. The majority of both Huns and Alans at this time fought as mounted archers. Using powerful composite bows they would shower their opponents with arrows, avoid close combat if it did not favour them and close in for the kill when it did. Later the Alans were known for their heavy armour so it is quite possible that, like other Sarmatians, a number of them fought as armoured lancers.

Given that the Gothic army at Adrianople was a conglomeration of several contingents with no single overall commander and no integrated command system it is perhaps surprising how well they worked together when battle was actually joined. Prior to the battle the separate contingents had more or less gone their own ways. When faced with the possibility of being picked off separately by Valens' army or standing together they chose the latter. The needs and aspirations of each group coalesced, which is more than can be said for the Romans.

The Roman Army

The *Notitia Dignitatum* shows that at the time of the Emperor Theodosius, just after Adrianople, the main central East Roman praesential army (*Praesentalis*, or 'in the Emperor's Presence') had been split into two equal forces of 21,000 men each at full strength. This split may have occurred when Valens marched west to confront the Goths with part of his army, leaving the rest to guard against any new aggression from Persia. We do not know how many men Valens had at Adrianople but something close to a praesential army is most likely although as in all armies, few units would be at their full theoretical strength.

A number of factors lead me to conclude that Valens had less than 20,000 men. When his scouts erroneously reported that the Goths advancing on Adrianople numbered 10,000 warriors he believed them. He called a council of war to help him decide whether or not to offer battle or wait for Gratian's reinforcements advancing from the West. If he had 20,000 men it is unlikely he would have prevaricated. With a 2:1 advantage, commanding the best troops the East Roman Empire could muster, against a rag tag bunch of migrants and refugees, it would have been a simple decision. Yet in the council, reported in detail by Ammianus Marcellinus, several voices urged him to wait. Victor, his *Magister Equitum*, supported by Richomeres, who had just arrived at Adrianople in advance of the western reinforcements, both advised him to wait. Richomeres showed Valens a letter from Gratian which counselled him to 'not rashly commit himself to the risks of a decisive action single handed'.

The fact that the issue was debated at all indicates that as Valens believed the Goths only numbered 10,000 men, his army could not have been much more than 15,000 strong. In the end 'the fatal obstinacy of the Emperor and the flattery of some of his courtiers prevailed. They urged immediate action to prevent Gratian sharing in a victory which in their opinion was already as good as won'. (Ammianus Marcellinus)

We know a fair number of the Roman units present at Adrianople from Ammianus' account of the battle and the previous campaigns. Valens' army probably included all the Eastern *Scholae* (mounted guards units) amounting to around 3500 elite heavy cavalry at full strength. Two units of line cavalry are also named: the *Scutarii* and *Promoti*, as are two legions: the *Lanciarii* and *Matiarii*. Several elite *auxila palatina* (palatine auxiliaries) also took part. The *Batavi* were held in reserve, the *Sagittarii Valentis* (foot archers raised by Valens) and the *Cornuti* (who had fought the Goths earlier in the campaign) were almost certainly present. These named units give us around 4500 cavalry and 4500 infantry on the assumption that full strength cavalry and auxiliary units had 500 men and the legions 1000–1500 men. Probably few of these units were at full strength and the bulk of the unnamed units would have been infantry legions and auxiliaries. If we assume something close to 15,000 men in Valens' army then it may have been composed of around 3–4000 cavalry and 11–12,000 infantry. Like the Goths, most of the infantry would have been close combat troops but they were supported by several units of archers who usually formed up behind the spearmen to shoot overhead or from the flanks.

This was an elite army of picked troops with many veterans being recalled to the eagles to take part in the campaign. Unlike the frontier troops or Lupicinus' Thracian field army, these men had not known defeat and no doubt they fully expected to utterly destroy the band of unwelcome migrants who had been marauding through the Thracian countryside for the past two years. Over centuries of Roman history there had rarely been any other result. When the Emperor himself led the best Roman troops against marauding invaders on home territory there could only be one outcome.

The Battle of Adrianople

So the stage was set for one of the most decisive battles of the late Roman era.

The Goths had intended to head for Nike, bypassing Adrianople to cut the road running south-east from Constantinople. This plan presumed that Valens would have been further to the west but he had withdrawn back to Adrianople and set up a fortified position just outside the city. Valens could no longer be bypassed and the Goths on the move with their long train of non-combatants would have found themselves highly vulnerable to a Roman counter-attack. Fritigern now had to either find a good position to fight from or withdraw back north to Cabyle. If he delayed too long there was a risk that Valens would be reinforced by Gratian and if that happened the Romans would be too strong to defeat in open battle.

Fritigern needed time to prepare and so he sent a Christian priest to Valens with a peace offering. He asked for the reinstatement of the original agreement made at the time the Tervingi had crossed the Danube two years earlier, giving the Goths land to settle in Thrace in return for military service and perpetual peace. Fritigern also sent a private note to Valens in which he hinted that he really wanted peace. All Valens had to do was to make a show of force to cower the other Goths after which he (Fritigern) would be able to persuade the others to come to terms. Possibly Fritigern offered these terms in all honesty. It would not have been the first time that the Romans had favoured one barbarian leader over others and perhaps he hoped to avoid conflict to emerge as the pre-eminent Gothic leader thanks to Roman patronage. On the other hand maybe he was only playing for time thinking he could defeat Valens but needing a pause to set up a good defensible position where his many followers would not be vulnerable to hunger, thirst and disease.

Fritigern's peace overtures were rejected and at dawn on 9 August 378, Valens left his baggage, the imperial treasury and his civilian councillors in Adrianople and marched out at the head of his army to engage the Goths. It was a blisteringly hot day and the terrain was rough and hilly. After a march of 13 kms the Romans came in sight of the Gothic camp. The location has been a matter of conjecture for many years but it could only have been either to the north or east of Adrianople.

German historians in the early twentieth century identified the ridge at Dermirhanli, 13 kms east of Adrianople (modern Erdine) as the site of the battle. This presumes that the Goths held firm to their original plan to strike for Nike and cut off the Roman supply lines from Constantinople. While the Dermirhanli ridge (which runs north-south) provides a good defensive position to attack from Adrianople to the west it could be easily outflanked to the south where the main Roman road lay and more importantly there are no good water sources or forage to sustain the Gothic army and their many non-combatants.

At the same distance to the north of Adrianople lies the modern hamlet of Muratçali which has a small stream running through it. To the south, east and west it is protected by high ridges and the Tundzha River is only 5 kms to the west providing ample water and forage. If you approach this position from Adrianople, the north-south running ridges and gullies makes it impossible to see anything in the Tundzah Valley to the west. From Muratçali looking towards Adrianople to the south you can see everything. I have spent much time tramping over the possible battlefield locations and have concluded that Fritigern must have had his camp at Muratçali and that Valens marched north from Adrianople to meet him.

Many accounts speak of the Romans encountering a Gothic wagon laager which is assumed to have been a perfect circle of wagons. Ammianus mentions this when he describes the Battle of Ad Salices. No doubt in open plains the Goths would have drawn up their wagons in a defensive circle but the terrain beyond Adrianople does not lend itself to this. Apart from the flat flood plain of the Tundzha to the west, the area is cut with steep north-south running ridges which are not suitable to such an arrangement.

I served in a modern tank regiment for many years. Benefitting from the experience of our forefathers in the Egyptian and Libyan deserts in the Second World War we would form an open laager with our tanks forming an outer square to protect more vulnerable troops and vehicles inside if there was no other cover. If, however, the terrain was closer, we would take advantage of it and position our tanks accordingly. I have no doubt the Goths did the same. In open country they would form a circle, but in undulating terrain, like that around Muratçali, they would have deployed to suit the ground. Probably the Goths would have set up their camp with small clan groupings of several wagons close to the water sources while others were deployed as barricades to block the vulnerable approaches to the camp.

It is often assumed that the Goths remained inside their wagon laager and fought from behind the barricade, but this is highly unlikely. Usual practice was to engage the enemy in the open and only fall back on the camp if defeated. Had the Goths remained behind the wagons they would have not only surrendered the initiative to the Romans but they would have been unable to use their preferred tactic of charging into hand to hand combat. It is far more likely that the Goths formed up, on foot, on the dominating ridge just south of Muratçali while the majority of the wagons were tucked away behind the ridge as a refuge for the non-combatants and baggage.

Marching up along the long ridge from Adrianople towards the Gothic camp at Muratçali the Romans began to deploy at about 14:00. It was a blisteringly hot day and after a 13 km march they must have been feeling a little worse for wear. In front of them they would have seen a line of Goths on the high ground blocking the approach to their camp. From the top of the north-south running ridge, along which the Romans would have marched, they could not see into the low lying Tundzha Valley to the northwest. This would prove problematic as not all the Goths were defending the approaches to the wagon laager.

The Tervingi were there but the Gruethungi, Alans and Huns were not. In all probability these groups were foraging along the Tundzha further north and had not yet linked up with Fritigern. This would explain why Roman intelligence had not yet discovered their existence and why Valens was acting as if Fritigern's 10,000 were his only opponents. As the Romans began to deploy, Fritigern played for time in order that the other contingents could make it to the battlefield. He sent envoys to Valens ostensibly to negotiate peace but as Ammianus recounts: 'The enemy deliberately wasted time so that their own cavalry, which was expected at any moment, might have a chance to get back while this sham armistice lasted, and also to ensure that our men, who were already exhausted by the summer heat should be parched with thirst. With this in view they fired the countryside over a wide area, feeding the flames with wood and other dry material. A further fatal circumstance was that both men and beasts were tormented by severe hunger'.

As the negotiations were going on, with both sides becoming hung up on matters of protocol, some Roman troops took matters into their own hands. The *Scutarii* (a cavalry unit) supported by archers, who may well also have been mounted, launched an attack on the Gothic lines. This force, which was commanded by Cassio and Bacurius, was most likely the Roman advance guard and it appears that their attack was impulsive rather than ordered. It is highly unlikely that cavalry and archers would have attempted an assault on the wagon laager. In all probability they were probing around to the west, looking for a weak point in the enemy defences and trying to see what lay beyond the ridge-line which blocked the westward view. Quite probably they intercepted the lead elements of the Alatheus' and Saphrax's force which was coming in from the northwest to reinforce Fritigern.

Whatever happened it is clear that the *Scutarii* and archers became involved in a scrap which was larger than they could handle so they beat a hasty retreat. 'This ill-timed attack frustrated [the negotiations]. In the meantime the cavalry of the Goths had returned with Alatheus and Saphrax, and with them a unit of Alans; these descending from the mountains like a thunderbolt, spread confusion and slaughter among all whom in their rapid charge they came across'. (Ammianus Marcellinus)

At this point Fritigern's Tervingi surged forward to engage the main Roman infantry lines while Alatheus' and Saphrax's mounted warriors engaged the Roman cavalry on Valens' left. It would appear as if the Roman cavalry had some initial success, driving the Gruethungi and Alans back to the wagon laager. This may have been because the Romans initially only encountered the lead troops who would have been in pursuit of the *Scutarii* and archers. As more Goths arrived on the field the Roman cavalry were driven back and panic spread amongst the ranks. The rearmost cavalry units, which should have been deploying out to support the left wing, turned and fled the field. This left the left flank of the Roman infantry open and exposed.

'Our left wing had advanced actually up to the wagons, with the intent
to push on still further if they were properly supported; but they were
deserted by the rest of the cavalry, and so pressed upon by the superior
numbers of the enemy, that they were overwhelmed and gave way like a

broken dyke. This left our infantry unprotected and the different com-
panies became so huddled together that a soldier could hardly draw his
sword, or withdraw his hand after he had once stretched it out. And by
this time such clouds of dust arose that it was scarcely possible to see the
sky, which resounded with horrible cries; and in consequence, the darts,
which were bearing death on every side, reached their mark, and fell with
deadly effect, because no one could see them beforehand so as to guard
against them'. (Ammianus Marcellinus)

Engaged in fierce hand–to–hand combat with the Tervingi to their front, the Roman
infantry line crumbled in on itself as the Gruethungi, Alan and Hun mounted
warriors charged their flank. Those who could fled the field but some elite units
made a last stand. Two of the army's most senior palatine legions, the *Lanciarii* and
the *Matiarii* held firm amongst the chaos and confusion. On foot, Valens sought
refuge amongst their ranks and sent Victor to call up the *Batavi*, who had been
placed in reserve. But the *Batavi* and the other reserves had already fled.

Valens did not survive. There are two accounts of how he met his death. One is
that he was killed by an arrow as he stood amongst the ranks of the *Lanciarii* and
the *Matiarii*. The other is that he was wounded by the arrow and was taken by
his guards and some eunuchs to a nearby farmhouse which had a fortified second
storey. When the Goths attacked the house they were at first driven back by archery
but then they set fire to it and Valens died in the blaze. One man jumped from a
window and was taken prisoner by the Goths and told the story.

Two–thirds of the Roman army died at Adrianople along with Valens, Trajan,
Sebastian and thirty–five tribunes. It was not Rome's first defeat at the hands of
Germanic barbarians and nor was it the first time an emperor had been killed
on the field of battle. Although Rome still had the resources to recover from the
defeat, the old pattern had been broken. It was no longer a certainty that the Roman
counter–attack would drive the invaders back to their homelands to re–establish the
status quo. Instead, although probably no one realized it at the time, a new status
quo had been established.

Gothic Warfare

What does the battle tell us about how the Goths waged war? A myth has sprung
up in modern times that Adrianople was a victory of cavalry over infantry and
therefore it resulted in the end of the Roman legionary and the emergence of the
mounted knight. Some modern accounts even erroneously credit the Gothic victory to the use of stirrups which would not be seen in Europe for a few more
centuries.

These misunderstandings seem to stem originally from the writings of Vegetius who in the fifth century lamented the passing of the old Roman military systems. They were perpetuated by Victorian historians such as Sir Charles Oman. Writing in 1884 Oman states that Adrianople was: 'The first great victory gained by heavy cavalry which had now shown its ability to supplant the heavy infantry of Rome as the ruling power in war. During their sojourn in the steppes of southern Russia the Goths, first of all Teutonic races, had become a nation of horsemen… The shock came, and probably to his own surprise, when the Goth found that his stout lance and good steed would carry him through the serried ranks of the legion. He had become the arbiter of war, the lineal ancestor of all the knights of the middle ages, the inaugurator of that ascendancy of the horseman which was to ensure for a thousand years'.

The majority of men on both sides at Adrianople fought on foot. While mounted warfare was becoming more important, both Gothic and Roman armies continued to rely primarily on men fighting on foot quite some time after the battle. As their fortunes improved, an increasing number of Goths would have been able to obtain and maintain good steeds but this did not make them exclusively mounted warriors. At Adrianople the quality of the horses the Goths had managed to round up from the Thracian countryside would have been marginal at best and probably used primarily for mobility rather than for tactical advantage.

The early twentieth century historian, Hans Delbrück provides a more realistic assessment of the post-Adrianople Gothic cavalryman: 'The cavalry was necessarily the arm to which they devoted all their care and attention, not in the specifically cavalry-related sense, but in the sense of the man who moves into the field on horseback knows how to control his horse and to fight from his mounted position but is also ready, if the circumstances call for it, to dismount and fight on foot. The warrior was not so much a cavalryman as a man on horseback'.

At no point at Adrianople did the Gothic cavalry charge into Oman's 'serried ranks' of well-ordered legionaries. They first defeated the Roman cavalry and then, while the legionaries were engaged frontally with the Gothic warriors on foot, they came crashing in on the flank. Rather than heralding a revolution in ancient military tactics, the Gothic mounted warriors were carried out a traditional cavalry role. Ammianus compares the Gothic victory to Hannibal's at Cannae. The comparison is apt because in both battles the Roman cavalry were driven off leaving the infantry to be hemmed in from both sides and slaughtered.

There would have been very little difference in the appearance of the Roman and Gothic armies which faced each other on that hot, dusty day in August 378. As we have already seen, Fritigern's force had completely re-equipped itself from the Roman armoury after Marcianople and his ranks had been swelled by Roman deserters and even formed Roman units. Although Alatheus' and Saphrax's men may have retained some of their native equipment, after two years campaigning inside Roman territory, much of what they had, would have been scavenged or looted from Roman sources. Both armies relied primarily on foot soldiers fighting in close combat with sword and spear, supplemented with javelins and supported by archers. Most of the cavalry were also equipped for close combat but both sides also had a number of mounted archers — Huns and Alans on the Gothic side and specialist units of *sagittarii* amongst the Romans. The Romans were trained and drilled to a standard that the Goths could not imitate but at Adrianople the tactical finesse of the Roman army did not stand up to the test. Deploying in multiple lines the Romans always maintained a reserve but when things began to go badly the reserve line melted away instead of restoring the situation.

What is most revealing about the Adrianople campaign is that it shows the strategic skill of the Gothic leaders and how well they managed to hold together their disparate followers for several years under very difficult circumstances. The Romans portrayed the Goths as wild, unruly, half-naked primitives with no real skill other than brute force and raw courage. Yet at Adrianople it was Roman troops who launched an impetuous attack without orders while the Goths maintained their positions. The Romans had a disastrous failure of intelligence, missing a size-able portion of the Gothic army while Fritigern, Alatheus and Saphrax managed to coordinate their actions despite the distance which separated their forces. Prior to the battle the Goths split into small bands to evade the Romans and to aid foraging and yet when the crunch came they were able to call the various groups together to concentrate their forces at the right time and place.

Fritigern must have been a man of enormous charisma and strength of will. He was able to hold together a confederacy of various nationalities with no greater authority other than their belief in his ability to win. His victory over Lupicinus at Marcianople would have established his reputation and as a result he was able to turn a miserable group of starving migrants into a well-equipped army. His various smaller victories in the skirmish actions that followed would have cemented his authority. Unlike the stereotypical barbarian he was shrewd, cautious and resourceful. Even Ammianus concedes this point saying that Fritigern had 'great foresight and dreaded the uncertainties of battle'. He only risked battle when he knew he could win and throughout the campaign he managed to maintain the initiative and make the Romans dance to his tune.

We know much less about the other Gothic leaders but the way the campaign unfolded seems to indicate that they too understood strategy as well as any Roman. At Ad Salices they made alliances with the Huns and Alans to break the blockade the Romans had imposed on them. After that they managed to stay out of harms way, find sufficient food to sustain them and inflict several defeats on the Roman troops operating against them.

The Aftermath

Against the odds the Goths had won but what was it they had actually gained? To be sure they had defeated the main East Roman army and as a result Gratian, who had been on his way to assist Valens, withdrew back to the West. The Goths now had more or less a free hand in Thrace but their position was still tenuous. They tried in vain to storm the city of Adrianople but the walls kept them out. Large numbers of Romans deserted to the Goths, including several *candidati* — members of Valens' inner bodyguard. Fritigern tried to use them to gain entry into the city by treachery but this also failed. Expressing the view that 'he had no quarrel with stone walls, he [Fritigern] advised the Goths to attack and pillage in perfect safety the rich and fruitful regions which were left unguarded. They approved of this plan, in which they knew they had the king's [Fritigern's] active support and advanced cautiously in small parties all over Thrace'. (Ammianus Marcellinus)

The Goths made an attempt on Constantinople but were overawed by the strength of the walls and deterred further by an unexpected sally by Arab mercenaries who were amongst the city's defenders. Ammianus gives us a colourful account of this engagement.

'They [the Arabs] are more at home in the tricks of guerrilla warfare than in formal battle but on the appearance of the host of barbarians [the Goths] they made a bold sally from the city. After a long and obstinate fight they parted on equal terms. But an incident of an utterly unheard of sort gave the eastern warriors the upper hand. One of them, a man with long hair wearing nothing but a loin cloth, drew his dagger and hurled himself with blood curdling yells into the midst of the Gothic host. He cut a man's throat, then he put his lips to the wound and sucked the streaming blood. This appalling sight terrified the Goths who lost their habitual confidence and advanced only with hesitation'.

Although the Goths had no imminent threat from any Roman army capable of defeating them, they still had a big problem. In many ways they were no better off than they had been in 377. They had to keep on the move to feed themselves but by this time there would have been very few farms left in the region which had been able to plant crops and harvest them. Meanwhile the walled cities were able to hold out against them. The Goths, now including a fair number of Romans, were farmers not nomads and they needed a place to call their own where they could till the land and feed their families. What they required was a peace treaty along the lines of the initial Roman offer back in 376 where they would provide manpower for the Roman army in exchange for land.

In the immediate aftermath of Adrianople it is not surprising that the last thing the Romans wanted was lots of armed Goths inside their territory. A wave of anti-Gothic feeling swept the East and fearing new rebellions, East Roman commanders massacred most of the Gothic soldiers still serving in the Roman army.

Therefore, the war dragged on for another four years. Gratian appointed Theodosius to succeed Valens as Emperor of the East in January 379 and he took over responsibility for dealing with the Gothic threat. He gathered new troops from Egypt and Syria as well as recruiting new non-Gothic tribes from across the frontier. Modares, a Roman officer of Gothic origin who had survived the massacre and remained loyal, led some successful counter-attacks. He drove his former countrymen further west into Illyricum where, once again, they split into smaller bands. Alatheus and Saphrax apparently struck north into Pannonia where they were checked by Gratian's western troops. Fritigern counter-attacked Theodosius' eastern army in Macedonia, driving them back to Constantinople.

With neither side able to make any significant headway the Goths and Romans finally accepted that negotiations were the only way to break the stalemate. On 3 October 382 a treaty was agreed which essentially confirmed the original Gothic aspirations of 376. The Goths were given land to settle along the southern bank of the Danube in return for military service. This service appears to have been the provision of recruits for the regular Roman army as well as an agreement that larger numbers of Goths might be called on for specific campaigns fighting under their own leaders.

On the surface this was nothing new. The Romans had a long history of settling defeated barbarians along the imperial frontiers as military colonists. This time, however, the Goths had not been defeated. All along they had been looking for a new homeland to call their own and although it had taken six years to achieve this they had won almost every engagement no matter how hard Roman officials may have tried to spin a different story of victory. Tens of thousands of Goths now lived more or less independently under their own leaders and laws inside the Roman Empire. The real significance of this was that the lesson learned by other barbarians over the frontier was that the old mould had been broken. No longer was it a certainty that an incursion would eventually be crushed with the dire consequences of a punitive Roman expedition into their home territory. The Goths had shown that it was possible to cross the frontier, defeat the best troops Rome could send against them and win a place to call their own inside Roman territory where they could benefit from all the riches that a more advanced civilization could offer.

Of course it was not quite as rosy as that for the new migrants. Like Syrian asylum seekers looking for a place in prosperous northern Europe today, the reality for transplanted peoples did not give them immediate access to the good life they might have imagined existed over the frontiers. Set up on marginal lands devastated by war the Goths did not find things quite as they had imagined it. In the years that followed this would lead to renewed conflict with Rome. In the immediate aftermath, however, they seemed more or less content to carve out a new homeland and provide military service as the terms of the treaty demanded.

Some modern writers doubt that there ever was a treaty in 382, claiming it is nothing more than a 'historian's construct'. In this version of events, having been broken up into small bands, the Goths were defeated piecemeal. Some were drafted into the army, others given patches of deserted lands to farm but there was no large group of Goths with some kind of privileged status living together under their own leaders inside the Roman Empire. It is true that there is no contemporary account of the treaty of 382 and that any details we have post-date the event. It is true also that contemporary Roman spin doctors, such as Themistius, did their best to dress things up as a Roman victory. If it had truly been a Roman victory then we might expect to hear of battles won and Goths being sold off into slavery or split up into small military colonies. However they are remarkably silent on such points. Indeed even Themistius has to admit that having tried and failed to win by force of arms, Theodosius had to resort to a negotiated settlement.

> 'He [Theodosius] was the first who dared entertain the notion that the power of the Romans did not now lie in weapons, nor in breastplates, spears and unnumbered manpower, but that there was need of some other power and provision, which, to those who rule in accordance with the will of God, comes silently from that source, which subdues all nations, turns all savagery to mildness and to which alone arms, bows, cavalry, the intransigence of the Scythians [Goths], the boldness of the Alans, the madness of the Massagetai [Huns] yield'.

The war ended with a whimper, not a bang, and there was no Roman victory. The Goths, one way or another, got what they were looking for in 376 — land in return for military service. The Romans, having initiated a war with the Goths, failed to defeat them in the field or to drive them back across the Danube. Theodosius was no doubt pleased to have a source of new recruits to fight his internal Roman enemies but it was hardly the outcome Valens was seeking when he marched west in 378. Whatever the terms were which ended the conflict in 382 the result was that an undefeated enemy had managed to wrest a piece of the Empire for themselves even if it may have been marginal land on the frontier and even if many Goths soon became dissatisfied with the deal. One way or another a new pattern had been set for the future.

Chapter 5

Alaric and the Sack of Rome

In the Service of Rome

The defeat of the East Roman army at Adrianople was a catastrophe for the Empire but as the fourth century drew to a close it seemed on the surface that Constantinople had managed to stabilize the situation. Fritigern, Alatheus and Saphrax passed from the record and we have no knowledge of what happened to them. Perhaps they died in battle or perhaps they were removed from power as a condition to Gothic settlement inside the Empire. Their followers seemed to have more or less settled down along the Danube frontier providing manpower for Theodosius to fight off various usurpers.

The Huns had made their presence known but, apart from a few small bands, they were not yet threatening Rome's borders and a new equilibrium seemed to have been accepted beyond the frontiers. Theodosius maintained a strong grip and was busy building a new Christian Empire. Things should have been looking up but with the benefit of hindsight we can see that Rome's situation was highly precarious.

In 383 Magnus Maximus (Macsen Wledig of Welsh legend) was proclaimed emperor by his British troops. With the backing of soldiers drawn from Britain and never to return, he defeated the Western Emperor Gratian, established his capital at Trier and for six years controlled the West. He was eventually defeated by Theodosius' Eastern army in 388 which included a sizeable contingent of Goths. How this might have been viewed by many Romans is preserved in a panegyric by Pactus:

> 'You [Theodosius] granted the privileged status of fellow soldiers to the barbarian peoples who promised to give you voluntary service, both to remove from the frontier a force of dubious loyalty and to add reinforcements to your army. They followed the standards which they once opposed. There marched under Roman leaders and banners the onetime enemies of Rome, and they filled with soldiers the cities of Pannonia which they had not long ago emptied by hostile plundering. The Goth, the Hun and the Alan responded to their names'.

Many Goths, however, seemed less than happy with being drafted en masse to fight in Rome's civil wars. They suspected that they were being deliberately sacrificed and that the Romans would dismantle the treaty of 382 if they got the chance. Some Goths rebelled or deserted rather than support Theodosius against Magnus Maximus and although this revolt was resolved through negotiations it was a precursor of what was to come later.

Amongst the Goths two factions seem to have arisen. On one hand were those who felt their future prosperity depended on keeping the treaty terms and finding accommodation within Roman military and political structures. Such men would have been courted by the Romans and would have advanced in power and prestige through Roman patronage. Many rose to high rank in the Roman army and later ended up fighting vigorously against their kinsmen. Others took a much dimmer view of Roman intentions and felt that they needed to look after themselves or risk having the fruits of victory being gradually whittled away.

Theodosius for his part did his best to keep the Goths on-side. He punished any Romans who wronged the Goths and he entertained the Gothic leaders, hosting dinner parties and giving presents. At one such dinner a fight broke out between two of the leaders of the rival Gothic factions. The pro-Roman Fravittas killed the Romano-sceptic Eriulf and as a result had to flee Gothic society with his Roman wife. Fravittas did well in the years that followed, rising to high rank in the East Roman army. Others, as we shall see, took up the anti-Roman mantle from Eriulf.

In 392, the new, youthful Western Emperor Valentinian II attempted to dismiss Arbogast, his *Magister Militum*. The result was that Valentinian died in rather dubious circumstances and Arbogast (of Frankish origin) placed his puppet Eugenius on the western throne. Once again Theodosius decided that he had to intervene to sort things out and once again he called on the Goths to back him. Some sources say the Goths provided 20,000 men and suffered 10,000 casualties. Such a large number is highly unlikely. If the whole Gothic army at Adrianople amounted to 15-20,000 men and Theodosius' Gothic contingent was drawn from their descendants then this would have been the entire manpower of the Goths settled inside the Empire since 382. It is unlikely that any treaty conditions would have required every able bodied Goth to join under the Imperial banner. Even if they had then it is just as unlikely that all would have answered the call.

Together with the Goths and reinforcements from Syria, Theodosius and his general Stilicho marched west in September 394 to defeat Arbogast in a two day battle that took place in a mountain pass in modern Slovenia through which the river Frigidus flows (modern Vipava in Slovenian or Vipacco in Italian).

Arbogast's army blocked the pass forcing Theodosius to launch a frontal assault. He used the Goths to do this and they suffered very heavy casualties without achieving any success. According to Zosimus, one of Theodosius' generals in charge of the barbarian auxiliaries was Bacurius — the same man who had led the Roman advance guard at Adrianople. If this is so then he must have been well on in years and it is ironic that he ended his career commanding the descendants of the men he had once fought bitterly against. Bacurius was killed on the first day at Frigidus as were many Goths. Theodosius unexpectedly won the battle on the second day aided by the defection of some of Arbogast's men and a 'divine wind' blowing into the faces of the West Roman army. Some historians claimed he had won a double victory. Firstly he defeated his West Roman enemies, secondly he had managed to kill off thousands of troublesome Goths.

In truth the Goths would become even more troublesome after the battle than before.

The Rise of Alaric

Theodosius' victory over Arbogast was won with the blood of many Goths most of whom would have been the sons or grandsons of those who had followed Fritigern across the Danube back in 376. One of the Gothic leaders who had survived the slaughter on the Frigidus, Alaric, then sought some better understanding for future relations. He had long been part of the anti-Roman faction and had taken part in the earlier mutiny when the Goths had been called on to fight Magnus Maximus. Given the magnitude of Gothic support to Theodosius, even if there had been far less than 20,000 warriors at Frigidus, Alaric appreciated that he and the other survivors of the battle were a force to be reckoned with.

With discontent brewing amongst the Goths, Theodosius died in 395, shortly after his victory over Arbogast. Flavius Stilicho became guardian of his 9-year-old son Honorius whom Theodosius had placed on the Western throne and his eldest 17-year-old son, Arcadius, ascended to the Eastern throne. As the vultures circled around the two young emperors Stilicho held supreme military power. His only real rival was Alaric who was now leading a substantial number of dissatisfied Goths.

As with the treaty of 382 there is a debate amongst modern historians as to whom Alaric was and his relation to the victors at Adrianople. Many of those who see the settlement of 382 as a Roman victory over scattered bands of Goths tend to view him as an opportunistic commander of mutinous Romano-Gothic troops with little connection to the followers of Fritigern, Alatheus and Saphrax. Those, including myself, who believe that Goths were not defeated in 382, tend to see him as a newly emerging leader of the anti-Roman faction amongst the Goths. The people he led onto Italy to sack Rome in 410 were the direct descendants of the victors at Adrianople, including Gruethungi as well as Tervingi. They were joined by others, including Romans, who flocked to Alaric's standard as his fortunes began to rise.

Despite attempts by Gothic propagandists such as Jordanes to give Alaric a royal lineage it is fairly certain that in 395 he had emerged as the leader of several thousand Gothic warriors who had served Theodosius but that he did not have any sort of hereditary right of rule over any other Goths. He had survived Frigidus and other survivors followed him. This was a strong base to build on and the death of Theodosius offered new opportunities.

Many times in the latter years of the Roman Empire we see cultural differences with regard to treaties. The Romans viewed the Empire as an enduring entity regardless of whomever happened to occupy the throne. For the Goths and other German peoples a treaty or agreement was between individuals. When Theodosius died, Alaric and many other Goths of the anti-Roman faction would not have seen any obligation to continue to serve Arcadius as they had served Theodosius. With Theodosius out of the picture the time was ripe for the Goths to try to get a better deal out of his successors.

There were plenty of conventional routes by which Germanic warriors could hope to achieve senior rank in the Roman army. Arbogast was a Frank. Stilicho's father had been a Vandal, Fravittas was rising up the ranks and Gainas, another Goth who had fought at Frigidus, became a powerful East Roman general. Yet Alaric's demands were different. He was not willing to rise up through the ranks of the imperial structures to become just another Roman general of barbarian origin. When he broke with the Empire in 395 he was seeking more than just power and a title for himself, he was also looking to become the recognized leader of the Goths and to re-write the treaty of 382 on better terms. In effect he was carrying on where Fritigern had left off.

Alaric led his men back to the East and there other Goths joined him although we have some indications that not all of them enthusiastically flocked to his standard. There were still a number of pro-Roman Goths who saw the future differently. Sarus, following in the footsteps of Fravittas, embraced Roman service. For many years he and his brother Sergeric pursued a feud against Alaric and his successors.

Be that as it may, by the time he was back in the Balkans, Alaric had a substantial force at his back and no Roman army capable of defeating it. Stilicho made a move to advance east to confront him but the court of the new Eastern Emperor Arcadius refused his help. They were more worried about Stilicho's threat to their power than any danger posed by Alaric's Goths. Yet the Romans could not possibly offer Alaric a new deal without risking the rise of a new usurper promising to crush the enemy. Therefore Alaric set his followers loose to raid and pillage not only the Balkans but Greece as well. They advanced as far as Athens and then carried on up the Adriatic coast availing themselves to whatever food, loot and captives they could get their hands on (see Map 6).

In 397 the eunuch Eutropius concluded a deal on Arcadius' behalf when Stilicho again made a move against Alaric's Goths. Rather than allowing Stilicho to become the power behind the Eastern throne, Eutropius granted Alaric what he wanted.

He was made *Magister Militum per Illyricum* (master of soldiers throughout Illyria) and his followers were given new lands to settle on improved terms. This was political suicide for Eutropius and two years later he was ousted by the Goth Gainas who had risen to the rank of *Magister Militum* following a more conventional route than Alaric. This left Alaric and his followers back in the wilderness, his agreement with Eutropius torn up and no immediate hope of new terms.

More Gothic Troubles

Eutropius' downfall, which ended his agreement with Alaric, was in part sparked by a revolt of yet another band of Goths. These were Greuthungi who had been settled in Asia Minor after a failed incursion across the Danube in 386. Unlike the victors of Adrianople they had been defeated and settled on the more usual terms of military colonists under Roman control. In 399 Tribigild, a leader of troops drawn from these Greuthungi, was rebuffed when he came to Constantinople 'to plead for higher office for himself and larger subsidies for his warlike nation'. This sounds very much like the same sort of things Alaric had been demanding and maybe Tribigild had been inspired by Alaric's rebellion.

A Roman Army led by Leo was destroyed by the Greuthungi when the barbarian auxiliaries in Leo's army went over to Tribigild and Leo failed to properly fortify his camp. The Gothic general Gainas used this as an excuse to set himself up as the Eastern Empire's most powerful warlord in emulation of Stilicho in the West. Gainas, who may have been a kinsmen of Tribigild, did not last long. He was overthrown by an anti-Gothic faction after accusations of collusion with Tribigild. Many of his Gothic troops and their families in Constantinople were massacred — 7,000 of them according to Zosimus. Gainas fled, pushed by yet another Goth in Roman service. This was Fravittas, the same man who had killed his rival at Theodosius' dinner party nine years previously. Tribigild's revolt was put down and Gainas escaped across the Danube where he was killed by the Huns and his head sent to Constantinople as token of good will. The strength of anti-Gothic feeling in the East was such that Fravittas' reward for his long years of loyal service was to be executed.

While Constantinople was grappling with Tribigild's Greuthungi and various Romano-Gothic warlords, Alaric and his followers stayed out of it. Probably he was relatively happy with his free hand in Illyricum and concentrated on building up his power base. With Eutropius gone and rising anti-Gothic sentiment in Constantinople he undoubtedly realised that new conflict was inevitable and his tenure in Illyricum was on borrowed time. Far better to consolidate his position rather than try to emulate Gainas and Fravittas as would-be Roman power-brokers. If Alaric came from the Romano-sceptic party amongst the Goths and if he indeed led a people rather than just a mutinous army, this would help explain his actions. He wanted formal recognition as leader of the Goths and a place within the Empire which his followers could call home, producing revenue and supplies. For a brief moment in 397 it looked as if he had achieved this but by the dawn of the fifth century the political situation in Constantinople had changed radically. Alaric's position looked increasingly tenuous.

Although there was not yet any direct military threat from the Eastern Empire, given the anti-Gothic sentiment in Constantinople, there was no hope of renewing the agreement he had made with Eutropius. In the autumn of 401, Alaric decided to break the deadlock by marching west into Italy to see if he could wrest a deal from Stilicho. It did not work. Two inconclusive battles were fought at Verona and Pollentia but Alaric needed a clear victory if he could hope to negotiate good terms. Without secure supply bases he could not remain in the field indefinitely while the well supplied Stilicho only needed to avoid defeat. Once again it was logistical weaknesses that proved to be the Goths' greatest enemy and so Alaric was forced back to Illyricum.

Illyricum (roughly the former Yugoslavia of modern times) was traditionally part of the Western Empire but it had been split between East and West to facilitate the joint campaign against Fritigern, Alatheus and Saphrax. It was the traditional recruiting ground of Roman armies since the second century and many soldier-emperors had come from there supported by the tough Danubian cavalry and legions. It was the bridge and the fault line between East and West. It has remained so into modern times when Croats, Bosnians and Serbs fought each other over more or less the same boundary that divided East and West Illyricum in the fourth century.

After Alaric retreated back into Eastern Illyricum, Stilicho began to formulate a plan to take the whole province back under Western control. This would give him greater access to the Balkan recruiting grounds and increase his power at Constantinople's expense. To do so he considered joining forces with Alaric who could then be pacified by controlling eastern Illyricum on behalf of the Western Empire.

> 'Stilicho, perceiving that the ministers of Arcadius were averse to him, intended, by means of the assistance of Alaric, to add to the empire of Honorius all the Illyrian provinces. Having formed a compact with Alaric to this purpose, he expected shortly to put his design in execution'. (Zosimus)

If this was indeed Stilicho's plan he was unable to put it into action. Developments beyond the Imperial frontier set a new chain of events in motion.

The Second Migration

Until the end of the fourth century the Huns remained mostly to the east of the Carpathian Mountains, enjoying the lands from which they had driven the Goths in 375-6. There were, however, signs that they would not stay there. Scattered bands raided across the Danube, others probed into Persian territory further east and still others served as Roman allies. Continued Gothic incursions after 382 may indicate that those who had remained behind in 376 were coming under increasing pressure from the Huns. By 410 the centre of Hun power had shifted to the plains of modern Hungary. As they gradually moved westward in the early years of the fifth century they set off a new exodus of Germanic and Sarmatian peoples.

The first wave of displaced migrants to break over the frontier was led by Radagasius, probably a Goth, who brought a large army into Italy in 405. The composition of Radagasius' force is not known but probably it was a coalition of various Germanic peoples and not only Goths. It included women and children as well as warriors, so it was a migration rather than a raiding force. Unlike the migration of 376 there was no attempt to secure terms with Rome — it was an uninvited invasion.

Radagaisus' army was large enough to require Stilicho to call up thirty Roman units as well as Hun and Alan auxiliaries to oppose the invaders. He also had to withdraw troops from the Rhine frontier to bolster his forces. According to the *Notitia Dignitatum* the Roman Army in Italy had thirteen legions, seven cavalry and twenty-one auxiliary units (see Map 2). At this period the cavalry and auxiliary units were about 500 men each while a legion contained between 1000 to 1500 men at full strength. Military units are rarely or ever at full strength but even so this should have provided at least 20,000 men and quite possibly more. Yet it took Stilicho a great deal of time to marshal the necessary forces — long enough for Radagaisus to ravage much of northern Italy. This shows just how misleading official army organizational lists can be. Unit strengths and levels of readiness can vary hugely and often only a tiny fraction of the theoretical military capability can be deployed. Just as Valens was only able to call on a small proportion of the vast array of troops serving the Eastern Empire in 376, so it was for Stilicho in 405, and would be for many others in the years to come.

In the end Stilicho decisively defeated Radagaisus near Florence on 23 August 406. Thousands of captives were sold into slavery, many others were drafted into the Roman army — 12,000 of the latter, according to Olympiodorus. Unlike the treaty of 382, this was how a defeated barbarian army was traditionally dealt with — no land settlements, no special treatment and no semi-independent status.

The Western Empire breathed a collective sigh of relief and Stilicho must have been feeling pretty pleased with himself. The barbarian threat dealt with, he fixed his attention back to the East, oblivious or unaware of a new storm gathering to the north and west.

Radagasius' following was not the only group of barbarians set on the move by the new westward expansion of the Huns. On 31 December 406 a coalition of Vandals, Alans and Suevi crossed the Rhine and spread throughout France. At the same time, there were several usurpations in Britain, the third of which saw Constantine III crossing the Channel in early 407 bringing with him the last remnants of the Roman army in Britain. He forged alliances with the Franks and Alamanni on the Rhine and fought against the various bands of Vandals, Suevi and Alans to bottle them up in northern Gaul.

Most of the military might of the Western Empire resided under Stilicho's command in Italy but he still had his sights set on the East and he underestimated the seriousness of the Vandal threat. Rather than forge a temporary alliance with Constantine to defeat this new barbarian incursion he sent Alaric's rival, the Goth Sarus, with an army to attack Constantine. A usurper was after all a far greater threat to his power than a mere barbarian invasion.

It all went wrong for Stilicho. Sarus was defeated, leaving Constantine in control of Britain and Gaul, with Spain also recognising his authority. Those parts of Gaul not under Constantine's control were overrun by the Vandals, Alans and Suevi. To make matters worse, Alaric decided that the time was ripe for another push into Italy. Stilicho decided that the best solution was to divert Alaric away from Italy and into Gaul so he convinced Honorius' court at Ravenna to grant Alaric 4000lbs of gold as protection money to spare Italy from another invasion.

Whatever kudos Stilicho may have gained from defeating Radagasius was rapidly being undone and the vultures closed in on him. In May 408 the Eastern Emperor Arcadius died. When Stilicho made plans to go to Constantinople to assert control, Honorius' advisors led by Olympius convinced the Western Emperor that Stilicho was planning a coup. Stilicho was arrested and killed on 22 August 408.

The Sack of Rome

With Stilicho suddenly removed from the equation, his agreements with Alaric were repudiated by Olympius. Therefore Alaric made good on his threat to march on Italy. On the way he was reinforced by many barbarian soldiers from the Italian army after their families were massacred in a wave of anti-barbarian sentiment which followed Stilicho's execution. 'Being highly incensed against the Romans for so impious a breach of the promises they had made in the presence of the gods, they all [the barbarian troops of Stilicho's army] resolved to join with Alaric, and to assist him in a war against Rome. Having therefore collected to the number of 30,000 men, they fixed themselves in whatever place they pleased'. (Zosimus)

Zosimus goes on to say that Alaric did his best to avoid conflict, preferring to persuade Honorius to honour the agreement Stilicho had made with him. Honorius' courtiers, dissuaded the Emperor from making any settlement with Alaric much to Zosimus' disgust: 'He [Honorius] ought either to have deferred the war, and to have procured a peace by a small sum, or if he preferred to contend, he should have collected together as many legions as possible, and have posted them in the route of the enemy, to obstruct the barbarians from advancing any further. He should likewise have chosen a proper person to lead them, and have conferred the command on Sarus, who alone was sufficient to strike terror into the enemy'.

When Honorius did none of these things, Alaric marched on Rome and seized the port of Portus which brought starvation to the city's inhabitants. Honorius meanwhile remained at Ravenna, his capital, protected by the surrounding marshes and waterways which made the city nearly impossible to take by assault. Without a decent general to lead his troops, Honorius made no move to relieve the Eternal City.

'Receiving no relief [from Ravenna], and all their provisions being consumed, the famine, as might be expected, was succeeded by a pestilence, and all places [in Rome] were filled with dead bodies... They [the inhabitants of Rome] then resolved on sending an embassy to the enemy, to inform him that they were willing to accept any reasonable conditions of peace, and at the same time were ready for war, since the people of Rome had taken up arms, and by means of continual military exercise were become well-disposed for action... After long discussions on both sides, it was at length agreed, that the city should give 5000lbs of gold, and 30,000 of silver, 4000 silk robes, 3000 scarlet fleeces, and 3000lbs of pepper. As the city possessed no public stock, it was necessary for the senators who had property, to undertake the collection by an assessment... The barbarians then departed from Rome, and pitched their camps in several places in Tuscany. Almost all the slaves in Rome then fled from the city, and enrolled themselves among the barbarians, to the number of 40,000'. (Zosimus)

What a humiliation this was for the city which had ruled the known world for more than half a millennium. Yet worse was in store.

Once Alaric had been bought off by the Roman Senate he sent bishops to Ravenna to plead for Rome's safety. In a scene worthy of a modern crime thriller where the mafia boss promises to 'protect' a business from destruction in exchange for a few 'modest considerations', the bishops 'advised the Emperor not to suffer so noble a city, which for more than a thousand years had ruled over great part of the world, to be seized and destroyed by the barbarians, nor such magnificent edifices to be demolished by hostile flames, but to prefer entering into a peace on some reasonable conditions'. (Zosimus)

Alaric's initial demands were to be given control of the passes of northeastern Italy along with modern Slovenia, southern Austria and the Dalmatian coast as well as 'a certain quantity of gold each year, and a quantity of corn'. This would have given Alaric a private fiefdom, cutting off all communications between the Eastern and Western halves of the Roman Empire and controlling the vital alpine passes. Honorius could not possibly accept this even if it meant sacrificing Rome.

The Imperial response was to agree to payments of gold and corn but that 'No dignity or command should ever be conferred on Alaric, or any of his family'. This set Alaric off to again march on Rome while the court at Ravenna did their best to find troops to oppose him.

With the soldiers of Stilicho's Italian field army having either melted away or gone over to Alaric, Honorius was forced to cut a deal with Constantine III in Gaul and recognize him as a co-emperor. He also sent for reinforcements from Illyria. 6,000 men answered the call led by a man with the unfortunate name of Valens. Alaric ambushed them, killing all but a few hundred who managed to make it to Rome. Zosimus tells us that Honorius also called 10,000 Huns to his assistance in the war against Alaric but nothing much seems to have come from this although a few hundred may have answered the call.

Alaric's next set of 'modest considerations' were to be given only the provinces of Noricum (roughly modern southern Austria) which his ambassadors pointed out were 'on the extremity of the river Danube, are harassed by continual incursions, and yield to the treasury a very small revenue'. He offered to waive cash subsidies as long as he got a supply of grain to sustain his growing number of followers. Holding to the time honoured policy of not giving in to terrorism or extortion, Honorius refused this reduced demand.

Roman emperors had always regarded usurpers as a greater threat than marauding barbarian armies and Alaric would have been well aware of this. When the Vandals and their allies invaded Gaul Stilicho had sent an army, not to attack them, but rather to attack the usurper Constantine who was actually holding them in check. So Alaric decided to set up a rival emperor of his own. In December 409 he set up the senator Priscus Attalus as West Roman Emperor — actually based in Rome. Attalus dutifully bestowed imperial commands on Alaric and his brother-in-law Athaulf but having done so he started to act with worryingly independent pretensions of real imperial power.

Key to the city of Rome's survival were the grain shipments from the fertile provinces of North Africa. Africa, however, was held by men loyal to Honorius. Attalus' general was defeated by the Count of Africa and when Alaric proposed leading his Goths to do the job properly, Attalus refused. Instead he insisted on marching on Ravenna with Alaric's Goths at his back to force Honorius' abdication. The arrival of 4,000 East Roman troops crossing the Adriatic by ship to land at Ravenna strengthened Honorius' resolve and made an assault by Alaric an impossibility.

Fed up with his puppet emperor not acting as a puppet, Alaric deposed Attalus. This re-opened negotiations with the court at Ravenna. There was no West Roman army capable of defeating Alaric in the field. Constantine III had the Gallic and British armies behind him but he was occupied by the Vandals as well as rebellious generals in Spain. With Eastern reinforcements Honorius was safe in Ravenna even if he did not have the strength to take offensive action. However, Alaric's position was precarious. He had to feed not only his army but also its many dependents. With the grain supplies from Africa under Honorius' control the possibility of starvation would have been an ever present worry. Alaric needed a settlement. He needed some concession from Honorius which would give him and his followers formal recognition and a base from which they could feed and equip themselves.

Encamped about 12 kms from Ravenna Alaric prepared to come to some sort of agreement with Honorius. This possibility was scuppered when Alaric's rival Sarus launched an attack. Sarus, also a Goth, had served Stilicho and had taken a different route to find fame and fortune. Quite possibly his attack was not sanctioned by Ravenna and may have been more about two rival Gothic leaders vying for supremacy rather than a loyal Goth in Roman service doing his master's bidding.

The result was that Alaric broke off negotiations and again marched on Rome. Extortion and negotiation having failed he had little choice but to make good on his threat to take the city. If he did not do so it would have been increasingly difficult for him to hold his followers together. Short of provisions and without any tangible benefit from their campaign Alaric's men would have soon taken matters into their own hands.

Although Rome was well protected by walls, the size of the city made it nearly impossible to defend without a decent determined garrison. Many sections of walls, built originally by Aurelian in the third century, still stand today. Although not of quite the same scale as the walls of Constantinople they are still a very impressive sight. However, nearly 19 kms of wall encompassing more than 100 square kilometres of city would have taken an awful lot of men to prevent a determined enemy from finding a way through or over. As far as we can tell Rome did not have much of a garrison and certainly not the numbers or quality needed to prevent Alaric's Goths from breaching the defences. Previously Alaric's tactic had been to strangle the city to gain concessions, now he was determined to take it.

So it was on 24 August 410 that Rome fell.

'Alaric had besieged Rome for two years successively, and Honorius, who then lay idly at Ravenna, had neither resolution nor power to relieve it. For being in nothing more unconcerned than in the safety of the city after the death of Stilicho, he had appointed no person to command the army and manage the war against the Goths. Perceiving that the Roman soldiers had either fled or were very negligent of their duty, the Goths decided to besiege the city. The barbarians having long endeavoured in vain and being unable to take it by assault, were obliged to have recourse to stratagem. They pretended to return into their own country, and selected 300 young men of great strength and courage, whom they bestowed on the Roman nobility as a present, having previously instructed them to oblige their masters by all possible observance. On the appointed day at noon... [the 300 slaves] met suddenly at the *Porta Avinaria*, where having surprised and killed the guards, they should open the gate for those who would be there in waiting... The Goths, on being admitted, immediately began to plunder the city, although they committed more dishonour than mischief to the citizens. It is the opinion of some, that the gate was opened by the contrivance of Proba, a lady of great rank and wealth, out of compassion for the people of Rome, who were dying of famine... Alaric made an edict that whoever took refuge in the churches, especially in those of Peter and Paul, should receive no injury; which was accordingly observed with great care'. (Zosimus)

Although it went on for three days, by the standards of ancient times, the sack of Rome by Alaric's Goths seems to have been a relatively restrained affair. Perhaps the greatest impact was psychological as the Eternal City began to look worryingly mortal. St Jerome wrote at the time: 'My voice sticks in my throat; and, as I dictate, sobs choke my utterance. The City which had taken the whole world was itself taken'.

Some pagans and less enthusiastic Christians expressed the view that Rome perhaps fell because she had abandoned her original gods. Zosimus even tells of pagan rites being allowed by the Pope in the desperate days of the siege as long as they were conducted in secret. Whether or not this happened, Saint Augustine took a very different view. He pointed out that Rome's old gods had not protected the city from its sack by the Gauls back in 390 BC. His opinion was that cities and empires rise and fall and the true struggle is between good and evil, not between competing earthly powers. Descriptions of Alaric's restraint and his protection of the churches may even have been added by later Christian writers to show that Rome's fall had nothing to do with the abandonment of the old gods.

The World Turned Upside Down

To many Romans in 410 it must have seemed as if the world had been turned upside down. The symbolic centre of the civilized world had been violated. That this could have been achieved by a bunch of savage, uncouth barbarians must have been nearly incomprehensible. Early modern views of Alaric's sack of Rome tended to see things in much the same way. At a time when European empires ruled the world it must have been hard to imagine how primitive tribes could capture the traditional capital of the greatest Empire the world had even known. '1163 years after the foundation of Rome, the Imperial City, which had subdued and civilized so considerable part of mankind, was delivered to the licentious fury of the tribes of Germany and Scythia... This awful catastrophe of Rome filled the astonished Empire with grief and terror'. (Sir Edward Gibbon)

In today's post-colonial world where former colonies have become great powers; where the armies of former imperial powers seem incapable of dealing with insurgencies in lands they once ruled; and where millions of migrants are risking all to seek new lives in the West; it is perhaps easier to understand what was happening in the fifth century. We can more easily comprehend the limitations of imperial power and we can also see that the divisions between 'civilized' and 'primitive' are not so clear cut as Romans or Victorian imperialists may have seen them.

Alaric's Goths were not the barbaric savages of popular imagination. In 395 Alaric started off with those survivors of the Battle of Frigidus who chose to follow him rather than continue to serve Rome. They were descendants of the men from various tribes who had defeated Valens at Adrianople. They had been living inside the Roman Empire for two decades, equipped and supplied from Roman sources and fighting for the East Roman Emperor. For a few years they had the status of a Roman army with access to Roman arms factories in Illyricum. Their ranks had been swollen by other Goths who would have seen following Alaric as a better option than remaining on the lands granted to them in 382. Other recruits came from Roman deserters and escaped slaves. Many men from Stilicho's army joined Alaric after Stilicho's murder and the massacre of their families in Italy. Quite probably many of these would have been the survivors of Radagasius' invasion so some would have been Goths but probably not all of them. The slaves who joined Alaric during the siege of Rome could have come from a wide variety of backgrounds and this documented reinforcement is unlikely to have been the only one.

Essentially, therefore, Alaric's followers were an army of mixed nationalities and backgrounds. They would have worn Roman clothing, been equipped from Roman arsenals and were seeking formal recognition for themselves inside the structures of the Roman Empire but on better terms than the treaty of 382 had given to the followers of Fritigern, Alatheus and Saphrax. They were not, therefore, simply the Goths settled along the Danube in 382 who had upped-sticks to move on in a second migration. Some of these Goths such as Gainas and Sarus had chosen other paths and they too would have had their Gothic and non-Gothic followers.

Modern historians debate whether Alaric's followers were simply an army looking for official recognition or a people on the move. The answer is probably a bit of both. While he may well have started off as a commander of Gothic troops in the Roman army, seeking formal military command for himself and his men, by the time he took Rome he had become 'King of the Goths'. Not every Goth followed him and many of his followers would not have had Gothic origins. His army had grown to essentially become a people and in the first decade of the fifth century they established a new identity that would eventually become known as the Visigoths.

Many or most of Alaric's soldiers would have had families and they followed their men as they moved back and forth between Illyricum and Italy. This had become the normal state of affairs. When the citizens of Constantinople rose up against Gainas they massacred many women and children who followed the men in his army. In the aftermath of Stilicho's murder the families of the barbarian soldiers in his Italian army were also massacred. It was not safe for Alaric's men to leave their families behind or they would risk a similar fate. Many of his followers had already experienced such horror. Therefore Alaric's army would have increasingly resembled a people on the move, the soldiers accompanied by women, children, old men and the infirm. This would have greatly compounded Alaric's logistical problems and limited his military options. His greatest difficulty was not how to defeat a Roman army but rather how to keep his increasing multitude fed and watered.

Interestingly, Alaric never defeated a Roman army in the field. He may have won the odd skirmish but the only formal battles he fought were a draw at best. His skills as a leader were in holding his people together, playing the political game and making sure that he was never put in a situation where he would run out of supplies.

So how many men did Alaric command? The short answer is that we do not know. Our only clue comes from Zosimus whose account of the first siege of Rome (previously quoted) tells us that the slaves who joined Alaric brought his forces up to 40,000. The passage could also be interpreted to mean that 40,000 slaves joined Alaric but such a large number seems highly unlikely.

20,000 soldiers was probably about the maximum that could be fielded in ancient times before the problems of feeding and supplying them outweighed any advantage of numbers. Larger armies could be concentrated for brief periods or with intensive pre-planning and pre-positioning of supplies. Without good supply sources large armies would have to be broken up into smaller groups to aid foraging just as Fritigern had to do in 376-382. There is no indication that Alaric broke up his forces prior to the sack of Rome although he and his brother-in-law Athaulf briefly operated separately. This would explain why, back in 401 when he failed to achieve a quick victory in Italy, Alaric had to retreat back to his supply base in Illyricum. If he had as many as 40,000 men at the various sieges of Rome he could not possibly keep them all together in one place before famine and disease would become a greater problem for the Goths than the Roman defenders.

Given the problems the Goths faced why was it not possible for the Romans to defeat them?

If we look at the Roman orders of battle of the time they should have had more than enough troops to deal with a few thousand mutinous Gothic allies in 395 and even enough to defeat an army of 20-40,000 when Alaric was besieging Rome. The Roman Army in Italy should have been able to field at least 20,000 men and a similar sized army was based in Gaul. Yet we know that Stilicho struggled to find thirty Roman units to fend off Radagaisus' invasion and had to call on Hun and Alan allies to bolster his forces as well as striping the border garrisons from the Rhine. The *Magister Militum per Illyricum* of the Eastern Empire commanded nine legions, six auxiliary and two cavalry units as well as nine units promoted from the frontier forces. This should have given a paper strength of around 22,000 men. The *Comes Illyricum* of the Western Empire commanded five legions, twelve auxilia and five units promoted from the border forces or around 16,000 men.

So what were all these men doing as Alaric moved back and forth between Illyricum and Italy? Alaric was given the post of *Magister Militum per Illyricum* back in 397 so for a time the troops of that command were his, at least for a while. It is highly likely that many of them would have stayed with Alaric when he marched into Italy rather than reverting back to Constantinople's control. Many of the men serving in regular Roman units were of barbarian origin. They would have had no more compunction in following Alaric than previous generations of Roman soldiers had in following various usurping generals.

If we think of the huge efforts it took by NATO nations and others to maintain relatively small numbers of troops in Afghanistan to deal with insurgents in modern times, then we have some idea of the problems encountered by the Romans in the fifth century. The situation facing the West Roman court at Ravenna was even more problematic. Only Italy and Africa remained under Honorius' control in 407-10. Britain, Gaul and Spain were either controlled by Constantine III or being overrun by the Vandals, Alans and Suevi. Before the sack of Rome Honorius and Constantine III briefly came to an accord and Constantine prepared to come to Italy's aid. Suspicion and intrigue prevented this from actually coming to fruition. The Eastern Empire did send troops to support Honorius but while they were enough to encourage him to refuse Alaric's demands they were not enough to allow him to take the offensive. Stilicho's army in Italy which defeated Radagasius could have checked Alaric as it did in 401 but after Stilicho's murder many of his troops deserted, many of them joining Alaric. Even if Honorius had been able to cobble together an army from various sources he had no general of sufficient calibre to hold them together and lead them to victory.

The capture of Rome was not Alaric's goal. He used the threat of it as a negotiating tool to extract what he really needed. This was a formal settlement with the Imperial authorities which would give him a new secure base from which he could feed and supply his followers. When he extorted huge payments from the senate he withdrew, distributing the wealth amongst his men and moving on to new un-plundered pastures. When it became clear that Honorius would not negotiate, Alaric did the only thing he could and that was to kill the hostage and take from Rome all she could give him.

This may have given Alaric wealth and prestige but he was still without a secure supply base. His men may have been laden with all the portable loot Rome could provide but they had nowhere to spend it. Furthermore the men, women and children who followed Alaric could not eat gold and silver. So Alaric moved south into the un-pillaged lands of southern Italy with the possible intent of crossing the Mediterranean, via Sicily, to seize Africa. At this time Africa was the breadbasket of the West Roman Empire, supplying the grain needed to feed the urban populations of Italy.

It was the Vandals, not the Goths who took this prize and Alaric did not live much longer after the sack of Rome as Jordanes recounts:

'At the extreme southern bound of Italy... which stretches out like a tongue into the Adriatic Sea... came Alaric, King of the Visigoths, with the wealth of all Italy which he had taken as spoil, and from there he intended to cross over by way of Sicily to the quiet land of Africa. But since man is not free to do anything he wishes without the will of God, that dread strait sunk several of his ships and threw all into confusion. Alaric was cast down by his reverse and, while deliberating what he should do, was suddenly overtaken by an untimely death and departed from human cares. His people mourned for him with the utmost affection. Then turning from its course the River Busentus near the city of Consentia... they led a band of captives into the midst of its bed to dig out a place for his grave. In the depths of this pit they buried Alaric, together with many treasures, and then turned the waters back into their channel. And that none might ever know the place, they put to death all the diggers. They bestowed the Kingdom of the Visigoths on Athaulf his kinsman, a man of imposing beauty and great spirit; for though not tall of stature, he was distinguished for beauty of face and form'.

Modern historians tend to discount Jordanes story of Alaric's burial as fiction. While Jordanes no doubt embellished his stories and made things up I am less inclined than most to dismiss him out of hand. Although writing more than a century after the fact, he was telling the story of the Goths as the later Goths themselves would have recognized it. Oral histories and traditions do tend to have their roots in some semblance of fact. Without more reliable sources or archaeological evidence to disprove them I believe we should give them consideration even if we do not take them at face value.

So what was Alaric's legacy? He will always be remembered by what was perhaps his greatest failure — the sack of Rome. His entry into the city was an admission of his inability to wrest from the Imperial authorities what he really wanted and his followers really needed. This was a permanent and powerful place inside the Roman Empire where they could enjoy the benefits of their campaigns in peace and security. Unlike Fritigern, Alaric never won a battle against a Roman army in the field but he had held the Empire to ransom and had risen from one of many Gothic nobles to become 'King of the Goths'. He must have been a man of enormous strength and charisma to hold so many followers together for so long despite all the many set-backs. His true legacy only became apparent after his death. The many people he had drawn to his standard were forged in battle to become the Visigoths who would eventually rule Spain until the Arab conquest 300 years later. He also set a pattern for the more immediate future. He had shown other ambitious men of barbarian origins that there was another route to power other than rising up through the ranks of the Roman military system. If you could gather enough good men behind you it was possible to make or break emperors and even make off with the loot the Romans had amalgamated over the preceding centuries. Before Alaric such a possibility would have seemed impossible. In the years that followed many others would follow in his footsteps.

Chapter 6

The Visigoths

From Italy to Gaul

Athaulf, Alaric's brother-in-law, took over leadership of the Goths and inherited the thorny problem of what to do next. With Ravenna in no mood to negotiate, the possibility of crossing to Africa scuppered with their ships and the Italian countryside ravaged by years of constant campaigning, the Goths needed a new plan. An opportunity was provided by a change in the shifting balance of power in the West Roman Empire.

By 411 Constantine III's grip on Gaul and Spain was starting to unravel. The Vandals and their allies had moved into Spain and Constantine's Spanish generals had risen in revolt. Constans, Constantine's son, was defeated and killed at Vienne and although Constantine managed to see off the rebels at Arles his control of the provinces he had ruled for the past four years was now much more tenuous.

The Emperor Honorius, meanwhile, finally appointed a general of sufficient calibre to take offensive action against the many threats to his authority — Constantius. He had several enemies to deal with. One was the Vandals and their allies in Spain, another was Constantine III based at Arles in southern France, the third was Athaulf's Goths in Italy. Given that the Goths had just sacked Rome; had more or less free reign in Italy; and had in their train not only Priscus Attalus but also Honorius' sister Galla Placidia, one would assume that the Goths would have been Constantius' first priority. They were not. Again showing how the Romans saw usurpers as a greater threat than any group of barbarians, Constantius left Athaulf's Goths in Italy and moved against Constantine at Arles. He was successful. Constantine was executed and after 4 years of semi-independence Gaul was more or less back under Honorius' nominal control.

In reality Imperial control seemed not to extend very far beyond Arles — the Gallic capital since the beginning of the fifth century. The lands on the west bank of the Rhine were now occupied by Franks, Burgundians and Alamanni while a colony of Alans had been set up around Orléans. Abandoned by the Imperial authorities and having to eke out an existence from lands ravaged by war, bands of disaffected Romans known as the *bacaudae*, had taken matters into their own hands. They controlled much of the northwest. No sooner had Constantine III been defeated than another usurper, Jovinus, raised his standard at Mainz supported by Burgundians and Alans.

Taking advantage of the situation, Athaulf led the Goths out of Italy into Gaul in 412. Probably bypassing Arles, which remained the centre of Roman power in Gaul, they made their way towards Narbonne. At first Athaulf made overtures to Jovinus and in doing so came once again into conflict with Alaric's old enemy Sarus who had been sent to Gaul by Constantius, possibly to negotiate with Jovinus. With only a small escort Sarus was ambushed, captured by Athaulf's Goths and executed shortly afterwards.

It seems as if Athaulf and Jovinus were unable to come to agreement so Athaulf switched sides. He sent an embassy to Ravenna offering to deal with the usurper in exchange for the elusive settlement which would give him and his followers a place within the Empire. Ravenna agreed and for a moment it looked as if the Goths would finally get what they were looking for. Athaulf's army defeated Jovinus, killed his brother and sent the usurper to Ravenna where he was duly executed. Things were looking up as peace negotiators went back and forth between Ravenna and Athaulf's base at Narbonne. But there was a problem.

Honorius' sister, Galla Placidia, was captured by Alaric during one of the sieges of Rome and had remained with the Goths ever since. Honorius wanted her back but Athaulf refused. According to Jordanes 'Athaulf was attracted by her nobility, beauty and chaste purity', and seemingly fell in love with her. Whether this was the case or whether Athaulf was seized with Imperial ambitions, he decided to marry her and Galla Placidia seems to have been willing. This scuppered the negotiations so Athaulf decided to flex his muscles and launched a sudden attack on Marseilles but was beaten back by Boniface, a Roman general who would emerge as a key player in the following decades.

Realising how much a usurper concentrated Roman minds, Athaulf once again proclaimed Priscus Attalus as emperor. Attalus had remained with the Goths even after Alaric had deposed him, no doubt feeling safer with them than facing whatever fate Honorius would have had in store for him. Attalus then duly appointed Athaulf as his *Magister Militum* and at some point the Goths expanded their territory to take Barcelona.

In January 414, at Narbonne, Athaulf married Galla Placidia. The ceremony took place in the house of Ignatius, a prominent Gallo-Roman with Attalus giving a reading. It was a Roman ceremony, conducted in Latin, linking the King of the Goths to the Imperial Theodosian dynasty. When a son was born to them he was named Theodosius in memory of his maternal grandfather. As Honorius had no heir, the baby Theodosius not only linked the Goths and Romans but also would have had a decent claim on the West Roman throne. The fifth century Spanish chronicler Orosius reported that Athaulf stated that he would use Gothic military power to uphold and defend the spirit of the Roman world. He put the following words into Athaulf's mouth which are probably more rhetorical than historical but they do convey a sentiment which seems to have been matched by some reality.

'At first I wanted to erase the Roman name and convert all Roman territory into a Gothic empire: I longed for Romania to become Gothia, and Athaulf to be what Caesar Augustus had been. But long experience has taught me that the ungoverned wildness of the Goths will never submit to laws, and that without law a state is not a state. Therefore I have more prudently chosen the different glory of reviving the Roman name with Gothic vigour, and I hope to be acknowledged by posterity as the initiator of a Roman restoration, since it is impossible for me to alter the character of this Empire.' (Athaulf as quoted by Orosius)

If Athaulf thought that this would give him legitimacy or a route to Imperial power he was mistaken. Roman fleets blockaded the coasts bringing famine and forcing the Goths to agree to a new accommodation with Ravenna. The baby Theodosius died in Barcelona and Athaulf was murdered in September 415. His assassin, with the appropriate name of Dubius, was avenging his former master who had been killed by Athaulf. 'For the master of this man was, of old, king of a Gothic troop, and had been slain by Athaulf'. (Olympiodorus). This 'Gothic King' may have been Alaric's old enemy Sarus although the fact that Olympiodorus does not name him casts some doubt on this possibility. Whether or not Athaulf's assassination was revenge for Sarus' execution, Sarus' brother Sergeric then staged a coup, slaughtered Athaulf's family and ruled for seven days before he too was killed and the Goths elected Wallia as their new king.

At first Wallia continued to oppose Constantius but the Roman naval blockade continued to make life very difficult and brought the Goths to the brink of starvation. After years of constant warfare the Gallic countryside was no better at supplying the Goths than Italy had been. In 416 Wallia made another attempt to move his people to Africa — the breadbasket of the West. Like Alaric's attempt six years earlier the plan fell apart when his ships were wrecked by a storm. Later that year Wallia made his peace with Ravenna, returning both Attalus and the widowed Placidia, and agreeing that the Goths would act as a surrogate Roman army in exchange for much needed supplies of grain. Once she returned to Ravenna, Galla Placidia was given over to be married to Constantius, a match she was apparently not very pleased with.

In 416 Constantius unleashed Wallia's now compliant Goths on the Vandals and Alans in Spain. These tribes had crossed the Rhine back in 406, ravaged Gaul and then since 409 had divided up most of Spain between them. They were no match for the Goths. Wallia's men defeated the Siling Vandals, captured their king Fredibal and sent him as a captive to Honorius. From 416 to 418 the Goths waged war against the new barbarian overlords of Spain with devastating success. As the contemporary Spanish chronicler Hydatius reports:

'The Siling Vandals in Baetica were wiped out by King Wallia. The Alans who were ruling over the Vandals and Suevi, suffered such heavy losses at the hands of the Goths that, after the death of their king, Addax, the few survivors, with no thought to their won kingdom, placed themselves under the protection of Gunderic, king of the Asding Vandals who had settled in Gallaecia'.

More than happy with the results, Constantius recalled the Goths to Gaul in 418 and gave them the province of Aquitania Secunda, centred on Toulouse and the Garonne valley. We have very little detail on the terms of this settlement. In all likelihood Constantius had no idea that he was creating what would become the Visigothic Kingdom. Most probably he thought he was billeting a Romano-Gothic army on relatively unimportant lands far from the centre of Imperial power where they could act as a bulwark between the rebellious *bacaudae* to the north and the remaining Asding Vandals and Suevi to the south.

Roman field armies of the time had no fixed bases. They were billeted on the local population and landowners might be expected to give up a third of their holdings to accommodate troops. This could come either from taxes or in actual real estate. In the case of the Goths in Aquitaine it is far more likely that they were given land rather than a grant of cash raised through taxation. Aquitania Secunda had not had recent Roman garrisons, and much of the land was probably deserted in the aftermath of the Vandal depredations and endemic civil wars. The Gallo-Roman landowners were in need of manpower to bring the abandoned countryside back to profitability, the Imperial authorities needed manpower for the army and while the Goths had manpower they lacked land and the means to sustain themselves. It was the best sort of deal possible — one which benefited both side equally. The Goths finally got their piece of the Empire where they could do more or less as they pleased. They paid no taxes, they could live under their own laws, be ruled by their own leaders and even if they technically owned only a third of the land it would have been more than enough to finally support themselves. The Romans turned a rampaging army into farmers who would make use of deserted lands to feed and provide for themselves without any drain on the Imperial treasury. In return they had a ready-made army they could call on to do their bidding and did not have to raise any additional taxes to pay for them.

This barbarian prisoner from the Arch of Diocletian is probably a Goth. His hairstyle with combed down fringe is very similar to later depictions and may be a fairly realistic representation of a Gothic warrior of the late third and early fourth centuries. (Deutsches Archäologisches Institut Rome)

A scene from the Ludovisi sarcophagus depicting a Roman victory over the Goths in the mid-third century. This earliest representation of Goths depicts both them and the Romans in traditional classical styles. In reality they may have looked quite different. (National Roman Museum)

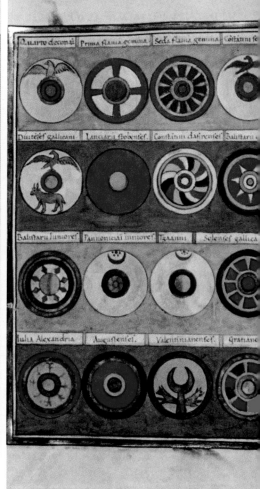

The insignia of the *Magister Militum per Thracias* showing the shield designs of the units under his command. These units were the first to deal with the influx of Gothic refugees in 376. (*Notitia Dignitatum*, Oxford Manuscript)

These two shield designs belonged to the Roman auxiliary units of the Visi and Tervingi. No doubt they were originally recruited from amongst the Goths. (*Notitia Dignitatum*, Oxford Manuscript)

The mausoleum of the Empress Galla Placidia in Ravenna. Captured by Alaric when he sacked Rome she married his successor Athaulf in 414. After Athaulf's death she returned to Rome and became the power behind the throne. (Author's photo)

(*Below left*) The treasure of Pouan was found near the 451 AD battlefield of the Catalaunian Fields. It was once thought that this may have been the burial goods of the Visigothic King Theodoric I. It is more likely that they belonged to of one of Attila's followers, possibly an Ostrogoth. (Musée Saint-Loup, Troyes)

The soldiers on the base of the Obelisk of Theodosius in the Hippodrome of Constantinople probably depict late fourth century Goths in Roman service. Their long hair, neck torques and lack of beards sets them apart from the short-haired, bearded Romans. An interesting detail is the fact that the shield bosses are off centre and the bottom of the shields seem to taper slightly. This may indicate a very early prototype of a 'kite shield' suitable for mounted action. (Author's photo)

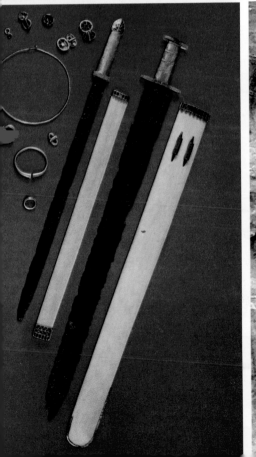

The belt buckle of St Caesarius who was Bishop of Arles 502-542, serving under both Visigothic and Ostrogothic rule. The soldiers probably represent Goths or Gallo-Romans who served them. (Author's photo – Musée de l'Arles Antique)

The signet ring of Alaric II the king of the Visigoths who lost his life and most of his Gallic territories to the Franks after the Battle of Vouillé in 507. (Vienna Kunsthistorisches Museum)

These Spanish re-enactors are equipped as typical late Roman cavalry. They could just as easily be Visigoths as their equipment and dress would have been very similar (Javier Gómez Valero)

A rare surviving example of a Visigothic sword and scabbard. (Author's photo – National Archeological Museum, Madrid)

As Goths were rarely buried together with their weapons, very few examples survive. This small collection of spear and arrow heads as well as daggers is in the Museum of Visigothic Culture, Toledo. Of interest are the two long thin spearheads which are not dissimilar to Roman pila and Frankish angons. (Author's photo)

A pair of magnificent gold and garnet Visigothic broaches which would have fastened a noblewoman's dress at the shoulders. (Author's photo – National Archeological Museum, Madrid)

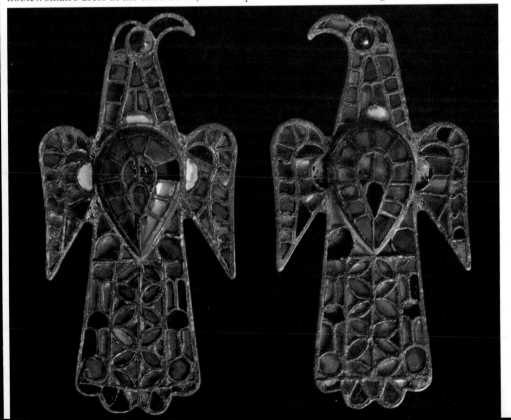

This detail from the Ashburnham Pentateuch illustrates a scene from the Old Testament. The dress and appearance of the figures could be that of sixth century Visigoths as the manuscript is thought to have come from Spain, although this is not absolutely certain. (Bibliothèque Nationale de France)

Many poorer Goths fought on foot as archers. If the Ashburnham Pentateuch is of Spanish origin this may be what a sixth century Visigoth archer looked like. (Bibliothèque Nationale de France)

A reconstruction of an early sixth century Visigothic warrior in the Toledo Army Museum. Like most Goths he has long hair and is clean shaven. His multi-part *spangenhelm* was a popular helmet style worn by Goths and Romans alike. He wears a quilted jerkin for protection, richer warriors would also have worn mail armour. (Author's photo)

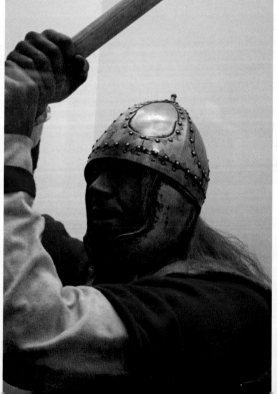

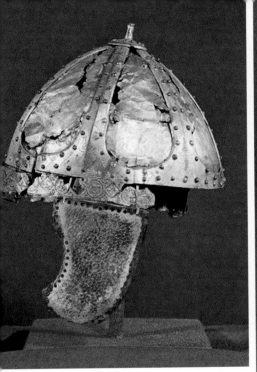

This *spangenhelm* style helmet from the end of the fifth century most probably belonged to an Ostrogothic warrior. (Vienna Kunsthistorisches Museum)

Very little Visigothic architecture survives. This pilaster turned into a pillar in the Church of El Salvador in Toledo is a rare example of their relatively crude artistic style when compared to that of the Romans. (Author's photo)

A Visigothic stone carving showing the baptism of a man with typical Gothic long hair style. (Author's photo – Museum of Visigothic Culture, Toledo)

This detail from the throne of the Archbishop Maximianus of Ravenna (545-553) shows East Roman soldiers. Their wide, decorated trousers were a style which may have been adopted from the Ostrogoths. The *Strategikon* recommends 'Gothic trousers' as standard military dress for East Roman soldiers. (Author's photo – Archiepiscopal Museum, Ravenna)

An elaborate Visigoth horse bit from Spain. Although their ancestors mostly fought on foot, by the time they established their kingdom in France and Spain most warriors would have ridden into battle even if they sometimes still dismounted to fight on foot. (Javier Gómez Valero)

A fine collection of jewellery and ornaments from a sixth century Visigothic noblewoman's grave in Segovia. (Author's photo – National Archeological Museum, Madrid)

The Pincian gate of Rome out of which Belisarius launched a sally against the Goths in 537. The impressive walls were built by the Emperor Aurelian in the third century. If properly defended as they were by Belisarius in the 530s they could keep an enemy at bay as long as food supplies held out and there was no treachery. Without a proper garrison to man the walls, as was the case in 410, they offered little protection. (Author's photo)

Ships in the port of Ravenna from a mosaic in the Basilica of St. Apollinaris Nuovo. Protected by marshes and easily re-supplied by sea Ravenna became the capital of the later Roman Emperors and the Ostrogothic kings. The Ostrogoths did build a navy but they were never able to match Vandal or Roman seapower. (Author's photo)

The man in the centre of this detail from the mosaic at San Vitale may well be Belisarius. The Emperor Justinian is on his left. (Author's photo)

These guardsmen in attendance on the Emperor Justinian are very similar in appearance those on the column of Theodosius. Their ethnicity is anyone's guess but it would seem that this 'Gothic style' of long hair with combed down fringes and clean-shaven faces had become some sort of universal military fashion which set barbarian soldiers apart from Roman civilians. (Author's photo – Basilica San Vitale, Ravenna)

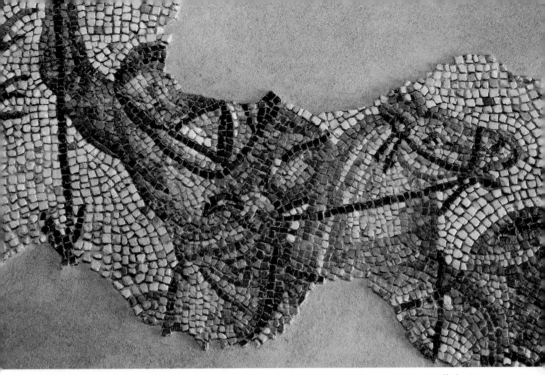

This mosaic fragment of a hunting scene from Theodoric's palace in Ravenna may well depict an Ostrogothic noble. The blue-grey around his neck could either be decoration or a cloak. (Author's photo)

Another mosaic fragment from Theodoric's palace shows a servant in very Roman-looking dress. He may well be a Roman serving his new Gothic overlord but it is also possible that he is a poorer Goth. (Author's photo)

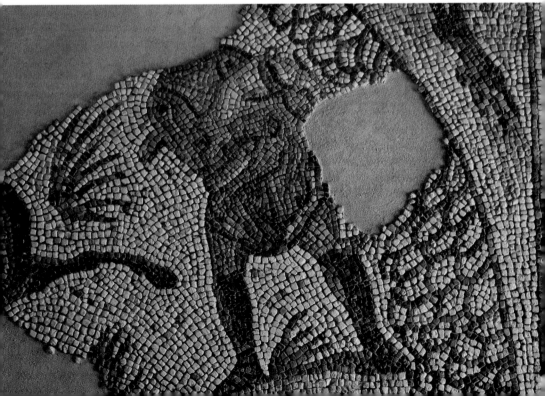

A pair of Visigothic signet rings now in the Madrid Archeological Museum. (Author's photo)

A gold medallion bearing Theodoric's image which is very similar to the mosaic from St Apollinaris. He is wearing armour, his hair is combed down in typical Gothic style and he appears to sport a small moustache without a beard.

This mosaic from St. Apollinaris Nuovo in Ravenna is thought to be a representation of Theodoric the Great in Imperial regalia. After the fall of the Ostrogothic kingdom a politically correct artist re-worked the original to portray it as Justinian. The man's broad face bears no resemblance to other depictions of Justinian but it is quite similar to coins issued by Theodoric. (Author's photo)

Theodoric's reign saw a brief flourishing of a Romano-Gothic society. He embarked on civil as well as military projects one of which was to renovate Ravenna's sewage system. His name on this lead pipe proclaims his good works. (Author's photo)

The remnants of Theodoric the Great's palace in Ravenna. (Author's photo)

This ivory from around 540 depicts several warriors in contemporary dress with wide trousers and elaborately decorated tunics. The two bearded men behind the throne are probably based on Lombards, the one holding his sword up looks as if he might be wearing a long sleeved mail shirt. The two men in front are more like Goths who were usually clean shaven. The moustachioed man, who is definitely wearing mail armour, could depict a Frank. (Author's photo – Archiepiscopal Museum, Ravenna)

Theodoric's mausoleum. In contrast to the other Ostrogothic buildings in Ravenna which are very Roman in appearance, this stands out as something quite different. Perhaps it was an attempt to give the king a more 'Gothic' last resting place. (Author's photo)

A warrior, probably serving in the East Roman army, using a two-handed lance without a shield riding down a dismounted man, possibly a Lombard. It is quite possible that some Ostrogoths also used this method of fighting. (Isola Rizza dish, Museo di Castelvecchio, Verona)

A manuscript illustration of the Third Council of Toledo in 589 when the Visigothic King Reccared abandoned Arian Christianity, uniting Goths and Romans in Spain under the same religion. (Author's photo – National Archeological Museum, Madrid)

A magnificent votive crown offered by the 7th century Visigothic King Recceswinth. This would have been hung above a church alter, not worn. (Author's photo – National Archeological Museum, Madrid)

The base of a column from the original Visigothic Cathedral of St Mary in Toledo. The inscription celebrates its re-consecration as a Catholic church by the Visigothic King Flavius Reccared in 587. (Author's photo)

This may have been the theoretical basis of the settlement of 418 but as we will see it did not quite turn out like that. Roman expectations in the fourth century were that temporarily successful barbarian incursions would at some point be defeated by the vastly superior Imperial armies and the barbarians would either be knocked back over the frontier with reprisals, or maybe the survivors would be dispersed and settled as military colonists. The Gothic victory at Adrianople changed this paradigm and the Roman failure to actually defeat the Goths in the following four decades consolidated the changes. By 418 there could no longer be a solution to the Roman-Gothic conflict other than finding a way to accommodate the Goths inside the Roman Empire as their total defeat had become an impossibility.

Gothic Military Power

At this point it is probably worth reflecting once again on the military prowess of Alaric's Goths and their immediate descendants. From a band of refugees who crossed the Danube back in 376 they had emerged to become the most feared and effective fighting force within the Empire. For forty years they had never suffered a serious defeat in open battle. It is true that they were often repulsed in their attempts to capture well defended walled towns although they did manage to take the greatest city in the known world. It is also true that Alaric was checked by Stilicho at Pollentia and Verona but he was not defeated and some contemporary sources actually claim these battles as Gothic victories. Ever since Adrianople the Romans had avoided open battle with the Goths as too risky. Far better to cut off supplies, starve them out and force them to move on. This strategy worked for Theodosius in the 380s and eventually worked for Honorius in the first decades of the fifth century.

With the exception of the drawn battles against Stilicho, whenever this group of Goths had the opportunity to engage their enemies in the open they invariably triumphed. This was true whether they were fighting on their own behalf or in the service of the Romans. The Vandals, Alans and Suevi had managed to overrun Gaul and Spain but when they encountered Wallia's Goths they suffered a devastating series of defeats which wiped out the Siling Vandals and decimated the Alans. What was it that gave the Goths such an edge?

It could not have been just a matter of manpower. Even if we assume that many of the Roman units listed in the *Notitia Dignitatum* were run down or lacking in enthusiasm it would have still been possible for the Romans to amass enough troops to match the Gothic numbers just as Stilicho had done to oppose Radagaisus.

We do not know how many fighting men Alaric, Athaulf and Wallia could command but it is possible to make a reasonable guess. Alaric had started out commanding some of the survivors of Frigidus after which he was joined by others who had been settled in the Balkans in 382. If we assume that at Adrianople Fritigern,

Alatheus and Saphrax had something close to 20,000 fighting men then the survivors who made their peace with Theodosius in 382 would have been somewhat fewer. At Frigidus, Theodosius is said to have had 20,000 Goths of which half became casualties. If this is true — and it is a big if — then Theodosius took with him every available Gothic fighting man. Those that followed Alaric in the immediate aftermath were only a small proportion. Gainas had been the overall commander of the Goths serving Theodosius and he went on to attempt other things.

So in his early days it is unlikely that Alaric had more than a few thousand warriors which possibly expanded to something close to 10,000 men once he had been joined by others and received his appointment as *Magister Militum per Illyricum* in 397. After Stilicho's murder Alaric was joined by the barbarian troops from Stilicho's army. According to Zosimus this brought Alaric's manpower up to 30,000 men. The addition of escaped slaves at the siege of Rome may have added another 10,000. Lack of supplies, with the inevitable death and desertion which followed, probably reduced the number of warriors over time but it is probable that Athaulf and Wallia could marshal something close to 30,000 men.

Nineteenth and early twentieth century historians often followed Tacitus to contrast the simple vigour of the Germanic peoples against the decadence of the Romans. Even if there was a tiny element of truth to this it would not explain how the Goths triumphed so easily over the Vandals nor how German recruits in regular Roman units might have been in any way inferior to the 'free' Goths. Some modern historians have speculated that the success of Wallia's campaign over the Vandals and Alans could have been due to being joined by Roman units from Constantius' army. As the Goths were acting as a surrogate Roman force in 416-18 this is a possibility. On the other hand our sources speak of 'Wallia's campaign'. If Romans had been involved, their commander would surely have been given precedence by Roman writers. In 422 the Visigoths were again in action against the Vandals but this time in clear support of a Roman-led operation. The Roman general Castinus is named in the sources while the Goths are simply anonymous auxiliaries.

If the early Visigoths had any martial edge over others, such as the Vandals, it probably came from the fact that for four decades they had been living inside the Roman Empire and on and off had been a pseudo-Roman army. Many men who joined their ranks had served in regular Roman units. At various times Alaric and other Gothic leaders held senior ranks within the Roman establishment even if such appointments had been fleeting. They would, therefore, have been familiar with Roman discipline and tactics and commanded troops who knew the same. In Illyricum, Italy and Gaul, the Goths would have been able to avail themselves of the armour, weapons and equipment from Roman armouries as well as from the battlefields. Compared to other barbarians such as the Vandals, the Goths would have been much better equipped, far better trained and had been forged by decades of constant campaigning. Compared to the Romans the Goths were not simply soldiers doing their duty. Their very survival and that of their families depended on victory.

Unfortunately none of the surviving descriptions of the battles and skirmishes fought by the Goths after Adrianople give us any detail. We can only assume that before 418 they still fought primarily on foot as most of their ancestors had and, indeed, as most Romans still did. From their settlement in the close country of the Balkans in 382 through their wanderings around Illyricum, Italy, Gaul and Spain the Goths of Alaric, Athaulf and Wallia would not have had any opportunity to build up a large supply of proper cavalry mounts. The only identifiable units of Gothic origin in the fifth century Roman army — the Visi and Tervingi — were foot soldiers of the *auxilia palatina*. At Frigidus Theodosius used the Goths to launch a frontal assault on Arbogast's mostly infantry army holding a mountain pass. This would have been a job for men fighting on foot rather than on horseback.

No doubt the Goths rounded up horses from the countryside and would have used them for mobility, foraging and skirmish actions just as Fritigern had. Maybe, following Roman practice, they might have kept a small mounted force as a reserve or to operate on the flanks. Certainly the leaders and their most notable followers would have had good mounts even if they dismounted to join their men in the front ranks as battle was joined. We have seen how the constant search for food and forage determined most of the Gothic actions between 395 and 418. Their problems would have been exacerbated if they had to feed and water a large number of horses as well as the fighting men and a large train of non-combatants.

So far from Oman's assertion that the Goths had become a 'nation of horsemen' (see Gothic Warfare, Chapter Four) it is far more likely that in the first decades of the fifth century most Goths probably still fought on foot with spears and swords, possibly supplemented with javelins and supported by archers. They would have been protected by large round or oval shields and by 418 many of them would also have been able to procure helmets and mail shirts. Wallia's army, therefore, would not have looked much different from Constantius'. Their weapons, armour and clothing would have all come from Roman sources. Even if the Goths had talented smiths they could not have done much more than repair damaged equipment as they were constantly on the move and a new sword, helmet or mail shirt required time to produce. Therefore the weapons and armour carried by most Gothic warriors would have come from Roman armouries, loot, or purchased with the immense wealth they had carried out of Rome.

Their Kingdom Comes

Between 418 and 450 Alaric's descendants built their power base in Aquitaine eventually coming to be known as the Visigoths. We do not know when this name came into common usage. Jordanes' account of an early division between Visigoths and Ostrogoths is anachronistic but the term *Visi*, or *Vesi*, was already being used by the Romans in the early fifth century and eventually came to be applied to those Goths who were settled in Aquitaine in 418 and from this point on I will now use the term to differentiate this group from the Ostrogoths who will shortly appear on the scene. These Visigoths were the descendants of many of the Tervingi, Gruethungi, Alans, Huns and Roman deserters who had fought at Adrianople. To these were added Radagaisus' survivors, the deserters from Stilicho's army, escaped slaves and others. Through forty years of campaigning to find a homeland they had forged a new identity which both they and the Romans saw as 'Gothic' even if not everyone could trace an ancestry back to those Goths who had crossed the Danube back in 376.

Theodoric, Alaric's illegitimate son, took over the leadership of the Visigoths from Wallia in 418 or 419. He set about realizing Alaric's dream by building a new kingdom on Roman soil, living relatively harmoniously with the Gallo-Romans of Aquitaine. Many of these Gallo-Romans would have found their circumstances enhanced rather than diminished by their new Visigothic rulers. The aristocrats continued to enjoy their cultured lifestyle and quite probably benefited from a reduction in taxation. The writings of Sidonius Apollinaris, a Gallo-Roman aristocrat who lived at this time, give us a sense of the continuation of a lifestyle that would have been familiar to Romans of Augustus' day.

On and off Visigothic warriors served as Roman auxiliaries such as the campaign against the Vandals of southern Spain in 422 and later against the Suevi in northwestern Spain. At other times the Visigoths flexed their muscles and tried to expand their holdings at Roman expense. They attacked but failed to capture Arles in 425 and again in 430. These may have been attempts by independent bands to strike out on their own rather than a deliberate effort by King Theodoric to expand his realm. The brief passage by Hydatius, which is our source for the latter attack, makes no mention of Theodoric, saying instead that it was a band of Goths led by a certain Anaolsus.

Between 436 and 439 the conflict between the Visigoths and Romans became more serious. By this time both Honorius and Constantius had died. Galla Placidia was ruling the West Roman Empire as regent to her son Valentinian III who had ascended to the throne as a 6-year-old in 425. The first Visigoth attack on Arles may, therefore, have had more to do with Roman politics at a time of transition rather than a deliberate move to break with Ravenna. In 429 the Vandals crossed into Africa and ten years later they captured Carthage and with it took control of the vital grain supplies to Italy. Real power in the West now lay in the hands of Flavius Aetius. He had been a hostage to Alaric's Goths as a child and had a Gothic wife. Later he was a hostage to the Huns and developed a special relationship with them. With the support of the Huns, Aetius built up his power base in Gaul, waging successful campaigns against the Franks, Burgundians and *bacaudae*.

We do not know the origin of the conflict between the Visigoths and Romans in the late 430s. It may have been brought about by Aetius attempting to assert more authority over the Visigoths. Many Romans beyond the Visigothic borders probably still saw them as little more than barbarian military colonists while under Theodoric's leadership they had evolved into an independent kingdom. Whatever the cause, the Visigoths took the offensive, again attacking Arles and laying siege to Narbonne. Aetius' general Litorius, with an army of Huns at his back, drove the Visigoths back to Toulouse and restored the status quo. During this campaign we learn of a fascinating incident when the Roman aristocrat and former *Magister Militum* Avitus, had to defend his Gallic estates from pillaging Huns in Litorius' army.

> 'Thus he [Avitus] spoke and bounded forth into the midst of the plain; and the barbarous foe likewise came. When first they approached, breast to breast and face to face, the one shook with anger, the other with fear. Now the general throng stands in suspense, with prayers on this side or that, and as blow follows blow they hang in the issue. But when the first bout, the second, the third have been fought, lo! the upraised spear comes and pierces the man of blood (the Hun); his breast was transfixed and his corselet twice split, giving way even where it covered the back and as the blood came throbbing through the two gaps the separate wounds took away the life that each of them might claim'. (Sidonius Apollinaris)

The image of a former Roman general (shortly to become emperor) fighting against Hun soldiers in a Roman army campaigning against the Visigoths, perfectly captures the confused loyalties of fifth century Gaul. Many Romans had become enemies of the state by joining the *bacaudae* to escape the heavy hand of taxation, while Roman armies could be made up of Huns, Alans, Goths or Franks. The Gallo-Roman aristocrats, such as Avitus, who found their estates in regions controlled by the Visigoths did not seem unduly perturbed by Gothic ascendancy. Not only did they make accommodation with the new overlords, many of them actively supported them. Some may have seen close cooperation with the Goths as a means to power or as a bulwark against the shifting politics of the Imperial court.

The Catalaunian Fields

In April 451 the Huns once again made their presence felt on the Roman and Gothic worlds. When Aetius's friend and ally Rua, King of the Huns, died in

433. He was succeeded by his nephews Bleda and Attila. Attila later murdered his brother and ruled alone radically changing Hun foreign policy. He prohibited Huns from serving Rome and in two campaigns against the Eastern Empire (441-42 and 447) the Huns devastated the Balkans and exacted an enormous tribute from Constantinople. With the East Roman frontier laid to waste and her cities looted, Attila began to look elsewhere for a new source of wealth and prestige. His eyes turned to the West. The reasons why the Huns suddenly turned against the West Romans with whom they had long been allies are complex and convoluted. A wide variety of causes, some quite trivial, sparked off the conflict.

First of these was the accession of the new Eastern Emperor Marcian in 450. He adopted a stronger policy towards the Huns than his predecessor Theodosius II. Marcian put a stop to the ruinous extortion extracted by the Huns in exchange for keeping the peace. Perhaps Attila's most obvious response would have been to renew war against the Eastern Empire but what would this have achieved? There was probably not a copper plate worth having anywhere in the Balkans that had not already been looted. Yet safe behind the walls of Constantinople the true riches of the East were beyond Attila's grasp. He could have sought to occupy land in the Balkans as the Goths had done in the previous century but after so many decades of continuous warfare the land was probably not worth holding.

Gaul on the other hand was still in contention. In addition to the Visigothic Kingdom, Franks held land along the lower Rhine frontier, the Alamanni were spilling over the upper Rhine and the Burgundians had been given land in what we now call Burgundy. Alans had been settled near Orléans, a band of Saxons were established nearby on the Loire and British refugees were moving into Brittany to join the *bacaudae*. Yet the Huns who had been such faithful allies of the West Romans still had no land within the Empire to show for their loyalty. From Attila's point of view a campaign in Gaul in which he might supplant one or other of the various petty rival kingdoms surely seemed a more profitable enterprise that once again descending on the Balkans.

A possible claim to a legitimate holding for Attila within the Western Empire came from a rather unlikely source. Honoria, the sister of the Western Emperor Valentinian III, became involved in a love scandal at court. Her lover was executed and Honoria was sent to be married off to a rather dull Roman senator to keep her out of trouble. In 450 Honoria appealed to Attila for help as her champion, sending him her ring as a token. Attila took this as a promise of marriage and demanded half of the Western Empire as a dowry. In moving against the West he could do so, not simply as an invader but as someone claiming his right as the Emperor's future brother in law.

Meanwhile the Franks, who had spilled over the lower Rhine frontier, were fighting amongst themselves over leadership following the death of Chlodio at the end of the 440s. According to Priscus, Chlodio's eldest son sought assistance from Attila to claim his inheritance. A younger brother sought help from Aetius who had adopted him as a son during an earlier Frankish embassy to Rome.

If these were not enough reasons to consider an invasion of Gaul, the Vandals in Africa were encouraging the Huns to move against the Visigoths. According to Jordanes: 'When Geiseric, king of the Vandals, learned that Attila's mind was bent on the devastation of the world, he incited him by many gifts to make war on the Visigoths, for he was afraid that Theodoric, king of the Visigoths, would avenge the injury done to his daughter. She had been joined in wedlock with Huneric, Geiseric's son, and at first was happy in this union. But afterwards he was cruel even to his own children, and because of the mere suspicion that she was attempting to poison him, he cut off her nose and mutilated her ears. He sent her back to her father in Gaul thus despoiled of her natural charms. So the wretched girl presented a pitiable aspect ever after, and the cruelty which would stir even strangers still more surely incited her father to vengeance'.

Concerned that Theodoric would lead the Visigoths against him to avenge his daughter's honour, Geiseric sought an alliance with the Huns. He probably hoped that if the Huns threatened the Visigoths the latter would be in no position to wage war on him. From Attila's point of view he possibly saw a great opportunity to supplant the Visigoths in southwestern Gaul while establishing a client kingdom of Franks in the north by supporting the eldest of Chlodio's sons. With Honoria as his wife he could have taken over the territories occupied by Aetius' enemies and continued the previous Hun policy of supporting the West with the added benefit of land within the Empire and a direct connection to the throne.

'Attila was of two minds and at a loss which he should attack first (the East or West Roman Empires). But it seemed better to him to enter on the greater war and to march against the West, since his fight there would not be only against the Italians but also against the Goths and Franks. Against the Italians so as to seize Honoria along with her money, and against the Goths in order to earn the gratitude of Geiseric, the Vandal king. Attila's excuse for war against the Franks was the death of their king and the disagreement of his children over the rule'. (Priscus)

When Attila made his move in the spring of 451 Aetius was in Italy and Roman Gaul was more or less undefended. Whatever remained of the Roman forces there had been run down or ignored for a generation. For more than twenty years Aetius had relied on Huns and Alans to secure his authority against the Visigoths, Franks, Burgundians and *bacaudae*. With the Huns suddenly his opponents, Aetius had to turn to the Visigoths for support.

Aetius called on Avitus to help him convince the Visigoths that they would be better off by throwing their lot in with the Romans rather than simply defending their territory. Sidonius Apollinaris gives a poetic version of Aetius' instructions to Avitus: 'Your influence alone is a barrier-wall to the Gothic people; ever hostile to us, they grant peace to you. Go, display the victorious eagles; bring it to pass, Oh noble hero, that the Huns, whose flight afore time shook us, shall by a second defeat be made to do me service. Thus he [Aetius] spoke and Avitus consenting changed his prayer into hope. Straightway he rouses up the Gothic fury that was his willing slave. Rushing to enrol their names the skin clad warriors began to march behind the Roman trumpets.' (Sidonius Apollinaris)

Supported by his subject German tribes, Attila marched east towards the Rhine in the spring of 451. Aetius, having secured an alliance with the Visigoths, moved north to stop him. The battle took place on the Catalaunian plains, five miles to the west of modern Troyes in Champagne. The Visigoths formed the right wing of the Romano-Gothic army, led by Theodoric, assisted by two of his sons Thorismund and Theodoric the younger. He left his youngest son Euric back in Toulouse. Thorismund led a Visigoth advance guard to drive the Huns from the ridge of Montgueux which dominated the ground to the east. The rest of the army deployed on the plain with Theodoric on the right, Aetius' Romans on the left and some Alans of dubious loyalty in the centre. Attila formed his Huns in the centre, with his Germanic allies on the two flanks. On Attila's right were the Gepids led by Ardaric and on the left were the Ostrogoths about which we will have more to say in the next chapter.

The Ostrogoths were led by the brothers Valamir, Thiudimir and Vidimir (there are other variations on the spelling). Valamir was the senior but it seems as though the younger brothers had a degree of autonomy. 'Valamir ascended the throne after his parents, though the Huns as yet held the power over the Goths in general as among other nations. It was pleasant to behold the concord of these three brothers; for the admirable Thiudimir served as a soldier for the empire of his brother Valamir, and Valamir bade honours be given him, while Vidimir was eager to serve them both. Thus regarding one another with common affection, not one was wholly deprived of the kingdom which two of them held in mutual peace'. (Jordanes)

Although the Ostrogoths were lined up opposite their Visigothic cousins, the Ostrogothic brothers owed their allegiance to Attila. 'They ruled in such a way that they respected the dominion of Attila, King of the Huns. Indeed they could not have refused to fight against their kinsmen the Visigoths, and they must even have committed patricide at their lord's command'. Jordanes goes on to say that Valamir was a good keeper of secrets 'bland of speech and skilled in wiles... Attila might well feel sure that they would fight against the Visigoths, their kinsmen'.

When battle was joined the Hun mounted archers drove back the Alans in the Romano-Gothic centre. They then turned their attention to the flank of the Visigoths which suffered from Hun archery and was in danger of being outflanked as the Alans retired. Meanwhile, the main part of their line had to face a succession of charges from their Ostrogothic cousins who were probably all mounted while most of the Visigoths would have been on foot forming a defensive shield-wall. Here shock action rather than archery would have been the order of the day. Armed with lances and javelins the Ostrogoths would have ridden towards the Visigoth line, hoping to break it by sheer force. If the men in the shieldwall held their nerve, presenting an unbroken line of spears and shields and closing any gaps as soon as they appeared, the horsemen would have been unable to break through. They may have exchanged a few blows with the front ranks of the infantry but then would have been forced to wheel back and rally for a second charge.

King Theodoric rode up and down the line to steady his men and keep the shieldwall intact as they faced the Ostrogoths while the Huns began to threaten their left flank. As he was doing so, disaster struck. 'While riding by to encourage his army, Theodoric was thrown from his horse and trampled underfoot by his own men, thus ending his days at a ripe old age. But others say he was slain by the spear of Andag of the host of the Ostrogoths'. (Jordanes)

However Theodoric died, his death might easily have caused his followers to break. They had been under terrible pressure. Nerves would have been stained almost beyond human endurance and the death of their king could have ended it. At that moment Thorismund intervened to save the day. Charging down the side of the ridge, probably on horseback, Thorismund's men 'fell upon the horde of the Huns and nearly slew Attila. But he prudently took flight and straightway shut himself and his companions within the barriers of the camp, which he had fortified with wagons.' (Jordanes)

The Visigoths and Romans had won the day but Theodoric was dead and his eldest son Thorismund was wounded. The Visigoths recovered the body of their fallen king and 'bore forth the royal majesty with sounding arms, and valiant Thorismund, as befitted a son, honoured the glorious spirit of his dear father by following his remains' (Jordanes). Thorismund was apparently dissuaded by Aetius from launching an attack on the Hun wagon laager to avenge his father.

> 'Aetius feared that if the Huns were totally destroyed by the Goths, the Roman Empire would be overwhelmed, and urgently advised him [Thorismund] to return to his own dominions to take up the rule which his father had left. Otherwise his brothers might seize their father's possessions and obtain the power over the Visigoths. In this case Thorismund would have to fight fiercely and, what is worse, disastrously with his own

countrymen. Thorismund accepted the advice without perceiving its double meaning, but followed it with an eye toward his own advantage. So he left the Huns and returned to Gaul. Thus while human frailty rushes into suspicion, it often loses an opportunity of doing great things.' (Jordanes)

Historians have debated the truth of this story for years but it could well be accurate as Thorismund's position was indeed precarious. Thorismund was killed two years later by his younger brother Theodoric II who in turn was assassinated by the other brother Euric in 466. So the heir apparent had every reason to depart the field quickly and get back to Toulouse to secure his throne.

The End of Empire

The Battle of the Catalaunian Fields found the Visigoths back at the centre of Imperial politics, this time in a position of strength rather than weakness as a new power vacuum was created in 454. The Emperor Valentinian murdered Aetius in 453 and he himself was assassinated a year later. Attila died in 454 and the Hun Empire fell apart as his sons and the subject Germanic tribes fought over the pieces. Secure in Aquitaine, the Visigoths were a powerful military force and several Imperial usurpers approached them for support, granting various concessions in return.

In 455 the Gallo-Roman Avitus was proclaimed emperor with the support of the Visigoths. He was deposed the following year by Wallia's grandson Ricimer who had chosen to rise up through the ranks of the Roman army. Ricimer had become the West's most powerful warlord, making and breaking emperors for the next two decades.

The Visigoths were given more or less a free hand in Spain and, probably with the support of the Imperial authorities, they destroyed the Suevic Kingdom in Gallaecia (encompassing modern Galicia, northern Portugal, Asturias and Leon). Jordanes says that the Visigoths were also supported by other barbarians: 'Making a compact with all the other tribes, Theodoric moved his army against the Suevi. He had as his close allies Gundiuch and Hilperic, kings of the Burgundians. They came to battle near the river Ulbius, which flows between Asturica and Hiberia, and in the engagement Theodoric with the Visigoths, who fought for the right, came off victorious, overthrowing the entire tribe of the Suevi and almost exterminating them'.

The Visigoths also expanded their territory in Gaul. In 462 Narbonne was ceded to them prompting a revolt by the Roman army in Gaul led by Aegidius. When Aegidius was defeated the Visigoths were able to expand north into the Loire Valley.

Many Romans gravitated to the Visigothic court, advising the king and helping the Roman way of life to continue despite the new overlords. In the 470s we even hear of Romans being granted senior military positions by the Visigothic King.

Sidonius Apollinaris wrote a detailed description of Theodoric II with whom he had good relations:

> 'He is well set up, in height above the average man, but below the giant. His head is round, with curled hair retreating somewhat from brow to crown... The eyebrows are bushy and arched; when the lids droop, the lashes reach almost half-way down the cheeks. The upper ears are buried under overlying locks, after the fashion of his race...his barber is assiduous in eradicating the rich growth on the lower part of the face...
>
> 'Before daybreak he goes with a very small suite to attend the service of his priests. He prays with assiduity, but, if I may speak in confidence, one may suspect more of habit than conviction in this piety. Administrative duties of the Kingdom take up the rest of the morning. Armed nobles stand about the royal seat; the mass of guards in their garb of skins are admitted that they may be within call, but kept at the threshold for quiet's sake'.

Apart from the 'garb of skins' which is either poetic licence or a reference to some sort of royal garb like the ermine worn by nobles in today's British House of Lords, this description conjures up images of a civilized king ruling over a civilized court. Theodoric was the sort of king men of refined tastes such as Sidonius could quite happily associate with. This would not have been the case back in the days of Fritigern. It is interesting to note that, in contrast to most Romans who had short hair and trimmed beards, the Gothic fashion was to go clean shaven with long hair. This style is confirmed by monuments and coins issued by Gothic kings — including the Ostrogoths. So far from being shaggy, uncouth, bearded barbarians, the Visigoths had developed their own style which still set them apart from the Romans but which owed little to their ancestral homelands beyond the Danube.

That the Visigoths were courted so assiduously by the Romans in the 450s–70s was in no small part due to the Vandals. North Africa was the breadbasket of the West and absolutely essential to Rome's survival as Alaric had learned. Now in the hands of the Vandals, with Vandal ships controlling the Mediterranean sea lanes, the survival of the West Roman Empire depended on getting it back. There was no love lost between the Visigoths and Vandals. Wallia's campaign against them in Spain and Geiseric's mutilation of Theodoric I's daughter had created a blood feud between these two Germanic peoples. With Wallia's grandson Ricimer now the power behind the West Roman throne, Imperial policy was to keep the Visigoths on side and focus on taking North Africa back from the Vandals.

In the end the policy failed. The Vandals sacked Rome in 455 and remained in control of the sea. A Roman fleet assembled on the east coast of Spain to invade Africa was destroyed by Geiseric's ships in 460 before it could set sail. In 468 the Eastern Empire came to the aid of the beleaguered West. Amassing a huge armada the East Romans set sail for Sicily where they were to link up with the West Romans and then strike for Carthage. This expedition was destroyed by Vandal fire ships at the Battle of Mercurium, off the tip of modern Cap Bon.

In the aftermath of the Vandal victory at Mercurium the Visigoths, Franks and Burgundians flexed their muscles in Gaul, expanding their territories confident in the knowledge that there would be no new army coming from Italy to oppose them. The new Visigoth King Euric (466-84) even sent ambassadors to the Vandals seeking to bury the hatchet after years of enmity, realizing that they were now a more important power than the rump of the Western Empire. Eight years later Odoacer, the leader of the barbarian troops of the Italian army, decided that he had no need to rule in the name of an emperor anymore and so did away with the fiction and ended the West Roman Empire forever.

Chapter 7

The Ostrogoths

Goths and Huns

When most of the Tervingi and some of the Gruethungi crossed the Danube in 376 many other Goths remained beyond the Roman frontier. We really know nothing about what happened to them or how they adapted to Hun hegemony. In 386 a band of Gruethungi made a failed attempt to carve out a place for themselves in Roman territory but were defeated and resettled as military colonists in Asia Minor. It was from this group that Tribigild rose to prominence and attempted to copy Alaric's bid for power (see Chapter 5, page 58, More Gothic Troubles). Many of the people who followed Radagaisus were probably also Goths. Yet many more remained beyond the frontier and only Jordanes tells their tale.

'It appears that at the death of their king, Ermanaric, [see Chapter 4] they… remained in their country subject to the sway of the Huns. Yet Vinitharius of the Amali retained the insignia of his rule… Disliking to remain under the rule of the Huns, he withdrew a little from them and strove to show his courage by moving his forces against the country of the Antes. When he attacked them, he was beaten in the first encounter. Thereafter he did valiantly and, as a terrible example, crucified their king, named Boz, together with his sons and seventy nobles, and left their bodies hanging there to double the fear of those who had surrendered. When he had ruled with such license for barely a year, Balamber, King of the Huns, would no longer endure it, but sent for Gesimund, son of Hunimund the Great. Now Gesimund, together with a great part of the Goths, remained under the rule of the Huns, being mindful of his oath of fidelity. Balamber renewed his alliance with him and led his army up against Vinitharius. After a long contest, Vinitharius [was defeated and killed]. Then Balamber… finally ruled all the people of the Goths as his peaceful subjects, but in such a way that one ruler of their own number always held the power over the Gothic race, though subject to the Huns'.

We really do not know how much of this is true. The fact that Gothic tradition recounts ongoing conflict between the Huns and Goths beyond the Roman frontier does seem likely. Just as likely is a power struggle between those Goths favouring accommodation with the Huns and those who still strove to oppose them. Part of Jordanes' purpose in recounting this tale may have been to glorify the Amal dynasty from which the kings of the fifth century Ostrogoths claimed descent.

When the Huns moved into the Hungarian plain in the early part of the fifth century we can only assume that some Goths moved with them while others remained behind. Of the latter we know that there were still Goths living in the Crimea long after the Huns had moved further westward. Of the former we are told by Jordanes that Vinitharius' three sons — Valamir, Thiudimir and Vidimir, led the Gothic contingent in Attila's army at the Battle of the Catalaunian Fields in 451. It is probably worth noting that only Jordanes' account says that Goths fought for Attila. The more contemporary Sidonius Apollinaris does not mention them at all:

> 'Suddenly the barbarian world, rent by a mighty upheaval, poured the whole north into Gaul. After the warlike Rugian comes the fierce Gepid, with the Gelonian close by; the Burgundian urges on the Scirian; forward rush the Hun, the Bellontonian, the Neurian, the Bastarnae, the Thuringian, the Bucteran and the Frank, whose land is washed by the sedgy waters of the Neckar'.

There is a huge amount of poetic licence in this description as many of the tribes Sidonius mentions had disappeared centuries ago and some are actually fictitious. His omission of Jordanes' Ostrogoths, therefore, should not be taken as conclusive but it does shed a shadow of doubt. I am inclined to believe that the brothers Valamir, Thiudimir and Vidimir did indeed lead a significant contingent of 'east Goths' or 'Ostrogoths' which formed the left wing of Attila's army in 451. In the conflict which followed the break-up of Attila's empire a significant body of Goths were active in Pannonia (the middle Danube) and would soon make as much of an impact on the Roman world as Fritigern and Alaric's Goths had previously.

The Hun Empire fell apart after Attila's death. His sons vied for control and the Germanic subjects rose in revolt. Led by Ardaric, who had held Attila's right flank on the Catalaunian Fields, the Gepids, supported by the Ostrogoths and other German tribes defeated the Huns at the Battle of Nedao in 454.

> 'There [in Pannonia] an encounter took place between the various nations Attila had held under his sway... Being deprived of their head, they madly strove against each other. They never found their equals ranged against them without harming each other by wounds mutually given. And so the bravest nations tore themselves to pieces. For then, I think, must have

occurred a most remarkable spectacle, where one might see the Goths fighting with lances, the Gepids raging with the sword, the Rugi breaking off the spears in their own wounds, the Suevi fighting on foot, the Huns with bows, the Alans drawing up a battle-line of heavy-armed and the Heruls of light-armed warriors. Finally, after many bitter conflicts, victory fell unexpectedly to the Gepids. For the sword and conspiracy of Ardaric destroyed almost 30,000 men, Huns as well as those of the other nations who brought them aid'. (Jordanes)

In the aftermath of Nedao, the East Roman Emperor Marcian recognised Ostrogothic control of Pannonia which previously had been ceded to the Huns. Constantinople also seems to have provided subsidies to the Goths to keep them on-side. According to Jordanes the three Ostrogothic brothers divided up Pannonia with each ruling a separate area but cooperating when threatened. The Huns were not so ready to give up Pannonia to their erstwhile subjects and continued to wage war against the the Ostrogoths in an attempt to reestablish their hegemony.

Probably aided by subsidies from Constantinople the Ostrogoths not only held their own but 'began to plunder the neighbouring races round about them'. (Jordanes) They defeated Attila's son Dengizich then turned their attention to the Germanic Suevi who still occupied territory to the west of the new Gothic realm. Many Suevi had immigrated to Spain along with the Vandals in the early fifth century but others had remained behind giving their name to modern Swabia. This conflict apparently arose when a band of Suevi crossed Gothic territory on their way to plunder Roman Dalmatia and in doing so appropriated some Gothic cattle. On their way back home Thiudimir led a surprise night attack on their camp and crushed them.

Sometime later, maybe around 470, the Suevi attempted to avenge their defeat and joined up with the Scirii (another Germanic tribe) to attack the Goths. In the battle which followed: 'King Valamir rode on his horse before the line to encourage his men, the horse was wounded and fell, overthrowing its rider. Valamir was quickly pierced by his enemies' spears and slain. Thereupon the Goths proceeded to exact vengeance for the death of their king, as well as for the injury done them by the Scirii. They fought in such a way that there remained of all the race of the Scirii only a few who bore the name, and they with disgrace. Thus were all destroyed'. (Jordanes)

Ostrogothic Warfare

A simplistic view of the fifth century Ostrogoths equates them with the fourth century Gruethungi and assumes a preference for mounted warfare for both. As we have seen in Chapter 3, page 22 (The Goths Beyond the Frontier) this is incorrect. Descendants of the Gruethungi ended up amongst both the Visigoths and Ostrogoths, while the Ostrogoths were not exclusively Gruethungi. It may have been the case that the Gruethungi, who originated further east on the steppes of modern Ukraine, would have been more adept at fighting on horseback than the Tervingi. Goths of both clans would, however, fight on horseback or foot depending on circumstances and the availability of mounts.

A preference for mounted warfare amongst the emerging Ostrogoths does, however, seem reasonable even if there is no hard evidence to prove it. Many had remained on the steppes east of the Carpathians under Hun dominion until the early fifth century when the Huns moved onto the Hungarian plain. There it was possible to continue to maintain sufficient horse herds to mount many men on good steeds. Most of the Gothic subjects were probably farmers, providing food as tribute to their Hun overlords but a warrior elite emerged who fought alongside the Huns. The Huns fought exclusively on horseback, primarily as mounted archers but also perfectly capable of closing into hand-to-hand combat.

It is reasonable to assume, therefore, that the Ostrogoths developed a preference for fighting on horseback on the steppes and maintained this as they moved further west with the Huns. The influence of the Huns and the neighbouring Sarmatians, both of whom were exclusively mounted warriors, would certainly have had an impact on how the Ostrogoths fought even if they did not take up mounted archery. Some modern historians have postulated that the Ostrogoths may have taken to using long lances in imitation of elite Sarmatian warriors who had been renowned for centuries for their ferocious charge. Such warriors used the *contus*, a 12-foot lance carried in both hands which precluded the use of a shield. The Romans created units of *contarii* (lancers) either in imitation of these Sarmatians or from Sarmatian military colonists. Units of *catafractarii* (heavily armoured cavalry) in the Roman army may also have been similarly influenced.

We will never know whether or not the Ostrogoths adopted similar fighting methods but it is certainly a possibility. A silver plate from Isola Rizza, near Verona, shows a sixth century warrior riding down an opponent using a two-handed lance. He is probably one of the *foederati* in the East Roman army and given the bitter war between the Romans and Ostrogoths of that time it is too much to assume that he is an Ostrogoth. It does, however, show that the Sarmatian-influenced style of fighting continued on well beyond the fourth-fifth centuries. It is also interesting that in his description of the Battle of Nedao, Jordanes mentions the 'Goths fighting with lances (*conti*)'.

The sixth century Roman military manual, the *Strategikon*, describes the more typical German way of fighting on horseback with spear and shield. It advises Roman cavalry to adopt their methods:

'They [the front ranks] then lean forward, cover their heads with their shields, hold their lances high as their shoulders in the manner of the fair-haired races, and protected by their shields they ride in good order, not too fast but at a trot, to avoid having the impetus of the charge breaking up their ranks before coming to blows with the enemy, which is a real risk'.

Probably most of the Ostrogothic warriors who followed Attila into France in 451 fought in such a way, armed with spears and shields, quite probably supplemented with light javelins. Jordanes says that at the Battle of the Catalaunian Fields, the Visigothic king Theodoric may have been killed by a javelin thrown by the Ostrogoth Andag. This combination of spears for close combat and javelins at a distance was the more typical way the various Germanic peoples fought on horse-back as opposed to the long *contus* of the Sarmatians. Procopius mentions shields and javelins being used by Ostrogothic mounted warriors in later battles. If some Ostrogoths took to using the long two-handed lance under Sarmatian influence, many others retained the more typical spear, javelins and shield combination.

Most lesser men, whose main role under Hun overlordship was to farm and provide food, are unlikely to have accompanied Valamir, Thiudimir and Vidimir into France in 451 — at least not in large numbers. After the break-up of the Hun Empire and the move into Roman territory these men would have accompa-nied the higher status mounted warriors, providing infantry support with some armed with bows and others with spears and shields. In the following century Procopius often mentions Ostrogothic foot archers and some modern historians have concluded that all the foot soldiers who accompanied the elite mounted war-riors were archers. There are however several descriptions of the Ostrogothic foot soldiers with spears and shields. It is possible that these could have been men who had horses dismounting to fight on foot, which most Germanic mounted warriors were perfectly happy to do. It is just as likely that not every Goth who fought hand to hand would necessarily have owned a good cavalry mount, especially in the lean years as Thiudimir's followers ranged through the Balkans and Macedonia.

My conclusion is that in the 450s there was an elite warrior class who fought mounted as Hun allies. Some of these may have favoured the two-handed lance but not all. They were still not cavalry as we now understand the term as they would dismount to fight on foot when the circumstances demanded it. The rest of the able-bodied males were farmers who could fight when called upon, those of higher status as spearmen and the poorer ones as archers. Breaking free of Hun control, every able-bodied man would fight. Those who could manage or afford it would acquire horses and might occasionally fight on horseback. Those who could not would fight on foot with a large number of them providing archery support. The warrior elite would have been well equipped, first from the booty of their raids into the East Roman Empire as Hun allies and later provided from the cash they received from the Romans as part of various peace settlements or from armouries that came under their control. Far from being 'skin clad' savages many of these men would have had helmets and body armour even if their poorer followers did not.

The Thracian Goths

While the Goths in Pannonia were busy fending off attacks from other tribes, relations with Constantinople were for the most part relatively peaceful. There was, however, a problem and that came in the form of yet another group of Goths who had been settled as *foederati* (federates) in Thrace. *Foederati* were barbarian troops serving in the Roman army in exchange for a combination of land and subsidies. Although the men were 'Roman' troops they fought under their own leaders rather than being drafted into regular units under Roman officers. These Thracian Goths had taken a separate path to those following Valamir, Thiudimir and Vidimir in the aftermath of Attila's death. At some point in the 450s they had been given prime land in the Thracian plain and received preferential treatment from the East Romans.

In the 450s Flavius Ardabur Aspar had risen to become the pre-eminent general of the Eastern Empire. His wife was the aunt of one of the leaders of the Thracian Goths — Theodoric Strabo (the squinter). Aspar used his alliance with this group of Goths to man his armies and maintain his power. In 457, with the Thracian Goths at his back, Aspar placed Leo on the East Roman throne and Theodoric Strabo became increasingly favoured at court.

This did not go down well with the Pannonian Goths. Even before Leo's ascension to the throne, Jordanes tells us of the rivalry between the two groups of Goths resulting in conflict. 'He [Theodoric Strabo] was allied in friendship with the Romans and obtained an annual bounty, while they [Valamir, Thiudimir and Vidimir] were merely held in disdain. Therefore they were aroused to frenzy and took up arms. They roved through almost the whole of Illyricum and laid it waste in their search for spoil. Then the Emperor [Marcian] quickly changed his mind and returned to his former state of friendship. He sent an embassy to give them the past gifts, as well as those now due, and furthermore promised to give these gifts in future without any dispute. From the Goths the Romans received as a hostage of peace Theodoric, the young child of Thiudimir'.

This settlement pacified the Pannonian Goths and gave them the means to successfully fight off the various other barbarian threats to their realm. There are indications, however, that Constantinople was increasingly worried about their growing supremacy in Pannonia. It was a time honoured Roman policy not to allow any barbarian group on the frontier to become too powerful and when it did they would support its enemies. According to the contemporary historian Priscus the Romans supported the Scirii in their war against the Pannonian Goths which resulted in Valamir's death.

Meanwhile, for much of the 460s the Thracian Goths seemed to be doing rather well for themselves under Aspar's patronage but as the decade drew on the political balance began to change. As it had been in the time of Alaric and Theodosius there remained a strong anti-Gothic sentiment in Constantinople. The Emperor Leo found a new source of military manpower amongst the Isaurians — tough men from the mountains of Anatolia. He promoted the Isaurian Zeno to counter the power of Aspar and the Goths, and in 471 he arranged for Aspar's assassination. Led by Ostrys, the Gothic troops stationed at Constantinople, rose in revolt. After failing to storm the palace they fell back on the Thracian countryside where they were joined by their compatriots.

At some point thereafter, Theodoric Strabo came to be the pre-eminent leader of the Thracian Goths. We do not know what happened to Ostrys, some modern historians have postulated that he may have been Theodoric Strabo's father. Whether or not this was the case, in 473, after threatening several cities in northern Greece, Strabo was able to extract a peace settlement in which he received 2000 pounds of gold per annum. This was a huge sum. By way of comparison, according to Priscus, the Pannonian Goths had received only 300 pounds per annum when they concluded their settlement with Marcian a decade earlier. Modern historians have calculated that 2000lbs of gold could have sustained 12-18,000 men for a year. Later, in 478 another treaty with the Thracian Goths specified enough gold to pay for 13,000 men. This gives us a good idea of the manpower Theodoric Strabo could command. In addition to this financial settlement, Leo appointed Theodoric Strabo as *Magister Militum Praesentalis* — Commander of the Armies in the 'Emperor's Presence'.

The Two Theodorics

In 471, as the Emperor Leo was seeking to reduce the influence of the Thracian Goths, he released Thiudimir's son, also confusingly named Theodoric, who had been a hostage at Constantinople for a decade. In the aftermath of Valamir's death, Thiudimir had taken primacy as the leader of the Pannonian Goths. His son Theodoric was the heir apparent. Now 18-years-old he was looking to make a name for himself as Jordanes recounts:

'So he [Theodoric, Thiudimir's son] summoned certain of his father's adherents and took to himself from the people his friends and retainers — almost 6,000 men. With these he crossed the Danube, without his father's knowledge, and marched against Babai, King of the Sarmatians, who had just won a victory over Camundus, a general of the Romans, and was ruling with insolent pride. Theodoric came upon him and slew him, and taking as booty his slaves and treasure, returned victorious to his father. Next he invaded the city of Singidunum, which the Sarmatians themselves had seized, and did not return it to the Romans, but reduced it to his own sway'.

Shortly thereafter the remainder of Thiudimir and Vidimir's followers joined in. By 473 they had become increasingly hemmed in by the Germanic Rugians who were pushing into Noricum to the west of their territory. Encouraged, or more probably angered, by the settlement Theodoric Strabo had managed to wrest out of Constantinople, Thiudimir's Goths took their chances by striking out deeper into Roman territory.

'Then as the spoil taken from one and another of the neighbouring tribes diminished, the Goths began to lack food and clothing, and peace became distasteful to men for whom war had long furnished the necessaries of life. So all the Goths approached their king Thiudimir and, with great outcry, begged him to lead forth his army in whatsoever direction he might wish. He summoned his brother [Vidimir] and, after casting lots, bade him go into the country of Italy, where at this time Glycerius [473-474] ruled as [Western] Emperor, saying that he himself as the mightier would go to the east against a mightier Empire. And so it happened'. (Jordanes)

Vidimir apparently led his followers across Italy to join up with the Visigoths in Gaul. Thiudimir and his son Theodoric once again invaded Illyricum with the majority of the Pannonian Goths and after taking Naissus they crossed the Balkans into Macedonia and northern Greece. A Roman army led by Hilarianus, met them at Thessalonica. When the Goths laid siege to the town and begun to construct circumvallations Hilarianus opened negotiations and bought off the Goths with gifts and land to settle in Macedonia.

In 474 Thiudimir died and his son Theodoric became king of those Goths who had followed him from Pannonia to Macedonia. Theodoric Strabo held sway over the other group of rival Goths in neighbouring Thrace. In that same year the Eastern Emperor Leo died and was replaced by the Isaurian Zeno. We have already seen how Zeno and his Isaurians had been used by Leo as a counterbalance to Strabo's Goths and his reign promised the demise of Strabo's power. Later in the year Theodoric Strabo supported Basilicus, the brother of Leo's widow, in a coup. Initially successful, Zeno was driven back to Isuaria, and Basilicus assumed the purple and Strabo was confirmed as his *Magister Militum*.

In 476, the same year that the West Roman Empire fell, Zeno was back in power after the non-Gothic troops in the East Roman army switched sides. Strabo lost his titles and his followers lost their lucrative payments from the Imperial purse. It seems that Zeno courted the other Theodoric (Thiudimir's son) and some sort of agreement was made with him when Zeno first ascended to the throne in 474. Those Goths following Thiudimir's son were moved by the Imperial authorities 400 kms from Macedonia to Novae on the lower Danube and Zeno transferred the post of *Magister Militum* from Strabo to Thiudimir's son, along with the subsidies Strabo had previously received.

Between 476 and 478 the Goths of the two Theodorics campaigned against each other with Theodoric Strabo achieving the upper hand despite his rival's Imperial backing. In 478 the Emperor Zeno proposed joining Thiudimir's son in a joint campaign to end Strabo's power once and for all. When the two Gothic armies came face to face somewhere in the Balkans, there was no sign of the Imperial reinforcements promised by Zeno to support Theodoric Thiudimir's son. In all likelihood Zeno deliberately withheld support hoping that the two troublesome bands of Goths would destroy each other and then he could intervene to wipe out the remainder. Instead the two Theodorics agreed not to fight. Feeling betrayed, Thiudimir's son marched on Constantinople but was repulsed. Zeno then concluded a new treaty with Strabo, giving him sufficient funds to maintain 13,000 soldiers.

Now it was Theodoric Thiudimir's son who was out in the cold without Imperial support. He led his followers back into Macedonia and then to the Adriatic coast where he took Dyrrhachium. On his way there his baggage train was attacked and captured by the Roman army of Illyricum.

In 479 an attempted coup by Marcian, grandson of the Emperor Marcian (450–457), changed the strategic situation. Theodoric Strabo supported Marcian but Zeno, backed by his Isaurians, defeated the usurper. As a result Strabo again lost his position and Zeno encouraged the Bulgars to attack them from across the Danube in 481. Although Strabo was able to see off the Bulgars he was thrown from his horse and died. Meanwhile Illus, another Isaurian who had led the Roman army which defeated Marcian, was making a bid for Imperial power. With civil war looming Zeno turned to Theodoric Thiudimir's son for support. In 484 he again appointed Theodoric as *Magister Militum* and also made him Consul. At the same time Strabo's son and heir Recitach was assassinated in a joint plot between Theodoric and Zeno.

Into Italy

After Recitach's death most, if not all of Theodoric Strabo's followers switched their allegiance to the other Theodoric. This probably brought together more than 20,000 Gothic warriors under a single leader. We know from various treaties that Strabo had at least 13,000 fighting men and that Thiudimir's son started off with 6,000 men on his own before being joined by the rest of Thiudimir's Goths. Suddenly the only surviving Theodoric had become the undisputed leader of a very strong fighting force.

This does beg the question why Zeno had conspired in Recitach's murder with the inevitable consequence of producing a single powerful Gothic army rather than two competing rivals? It was the same decision Honorius made when he saw Constantine III as a greater threat than the Alaric's Goths or the Vandals. With hindsight we might see such decisions as ultimately bringing about the Roman Empire's destruction. From the point of view of Zeno or Honorius, a usurper was always a much greater threat than a band of ravaging barbarians. A usurper could overthrow the Emperor while the barbarians would merely inconvenience the provincial citizens.

So it was that in 484, with the support of Theodoric's Goths, Zeno was able to defeat his rival Illus. Yet all was not well between Zeno and Theodoric. Mutual distrust led to a breakdown in relations and two years later Theodoric rebelled. He ravaged Thrace (yet again) and threatened Constantinople. Zeno bought him off with the usual gifts and then, in 488, came up with a cunning plan.

Since 476 Italy had been under the control of Odoacer, the leader of the barbarian troops of the Italian army. The Eastern Empire never recognized Odoacer's control of Italy, presumably accepting his rule as an interregnum after which it was assumed that a suitable emperor would once again ascend the West Roman throne. What better solution could there be to Zeno's perennial Gothic problem than to unleash the now united Ostrogoths as a surrogate Roman army to unseat Odoacer?

So it was, in autumn 488 that Theodoric, now a Roman Patrician with the official position of *Magister Militum Praesentalis*, led an army in the service of the East Roman Emperor to bring Italy back under Imperial control. So it was too that the same Theodoric, King of the Ostrogoths, led his people to new lands. The first was the fiction the courtiers in Constantinople hoped for and maybe believed. The second was the reality. As the sixth century historian Procopius recounts: 'With Theodoric went the people of the Goths, putting their wives and children and as much of their furniture as they could take with them in their wagons'.

Like Alaric before him. Theodoric was leaving the intrigues of the Eastern Empire behind to find new possibilities in the West. Unlike Alaric he had official sanction from Constantinople and there was no longer a residual Western Empire to oppose him. Yet it was not an easy march from the Balkans into Italy. Leaving late in the year with at least 20,000 warriors and their many more wives, children, old men and slaves, the huge Ostrogothic host had to overcome enormous logistical problems. Cities barred their gates so the Goths had to live off the land which had been ravaged by previous decades of constant warfare. On the Ulca River near Cibalae (Vinkovci in modern Croatia) their path was blocked by an army of Gepids, the Ostrogoths' erstwhile allies on the Catalaunian Fields and at Neado. In a fierce all-day battle the Ostrogoths eventually broke through the Gepid lines, captured their baggage train and, with it, enough food to push on.

It was not until the spring of 489 that Theodoric's advance guard was able to cross the Julian Alps into Italy and it took many more months for all his supply wagons to catch up. This left Odoacer time to prepare. In late summer Theodoric forced a crossing of the Isonzo River but failed to win a clear victory over Odoacer who fell back on Verona. In September Theodoric drove Odoacer out of the Po Valley towards Como but had to divert his attention to deal with an incursion by the Burgundians. The following year Theodoric defeated Odoacer on the Addua River, possibly assisted by Visigoth allies.

Odoacer then retreated to Ravenna where, protected by the surrounding marshes and able to re-supply by sea, he was impervious to attack. Theodoric established siege lines but Odoacer held out. At some point in 491 he was reinforced, presumably by sea, by some Herul allies. Together, in July 491, they made a sally but were driven back by the Ostrogoths. Odoacer then made overtures for peace and Theodoric accepted him as co-ruler of Italy in exchange for the surrender of Ravenna. The marriage of convenience did not last long. In March 493 Theodoric invited Odoacer to a feast and there he killed him. According to legend Theodoric cut Odoacer in half with his sword.

Whatever deal had been concocted between Zeno and Theodoric when the former let loose the Ostrogoths on Odoacer, Theodoric was now the undisputed ruler of Italy and was not in any mood to hand it back over to the Imperial authorities. As the sixth century historian Procopius reports: 'After gaining the adherence of such of the hostile barbarians as chanced to survive, he [Theodoric] secured the supremacy over both Goths and Italians. And though he did not claim the right to assume either the garb or the name of Emperor of the Romans, but was called *Rex* [King] to the end of his life for thus the barbarians are accustomed to call their leaders'. Zeno died in 491 so it was up to the new emperor, Anastasius to come to terms with the new status quo which made Theodoric not only King of the Ostrogoths but also King of the Romans.

So it was that as the turbulent fifth century drew to a close the Visigoths held much of southern France and northern Spain while the Ostrogoths held Italy. The West Roman Empire no longer existed and the Eastern Empire was apparently unable or unwilling to do anything about it. For a brief period these two Gothic kingdoms flourished, promising a new beginning which would merge Germanic and Roman culture. As we shall see, it did not quite turn out like that.

Chapter 8

The Gothic Kingdoms

The End of the Visigoths in Gaul

As Theodoric was establishing his authority in Italy, he cemented an alliance with the Visigoths by marrying his daughter Theodichusa off to their King Alaric II (484-507). The Visigoths, meanwhile, were expanding into Spain to occupy the vacuum left by their destruction of the Suevi and the end of the West Roman Empire (see Chapter 7, The End of Empire).

We only have scant hints at this further expansion. The Zaragoza Chronicle has a brief entry in 494 which simply states 'the Goths entered Spain'. A second entry for 497 adds: 'the Goths acquired settlements in Spain'.

As far as we can tell this further expansion into Spain was not a deliberate shift away from the Visigothic power centre in Aquitaine. More probably it was the result of younger warriors and those less favoured, striking out on their own to seek greater glory and riches. The royal court remained at Toulouse and seems to have had its work cut out to impose authority. The chronicles mention 'tyrants' setting themselves up in various parts of Spain. A certain Burdunellus was brought to heel, captured and sent to Toulouse. There he was placed inside a bronze bull and burned to death as an exemplary example to those who might make a bid for local autonomy. Clearly the Goths had learned much from the Roman obsession with usurpers and had come a long way from Tactius' descriptions of an egalitarian Germanic society.

As the Visigoths were thinning out into Spain trouble was brewing to the north. In 486 Clovis, leader of one of many Frankish bands on the upper Rhine, succeeded in defeating Syagrius who ruled the last remaining Roman enclave in northern Gaul. After this Clovis established primacy over the Franks, took over the Alamannic territories on the west bank of the lower Rhine and then continued on to reduce the Kingdom of the Burgundians with the support of both the Visigoths and Ostrogoths.

Whatever alliance the Goths had with the Franks it broke down in 507 when Clovis made a bid to expand into Visigothic territory. Alaric sent urgent pleas for help to Theodoric the Ostrogoth while doing his best to delay the Franks. In a letter preserved in Cassiodorus' *Variae*, Theodoric gave the following reply to Alaric:

'Surrounded as you are by an innumerable multitude of subjects, and strong in the remembrance of their having turned back Attila, still do not fight with Clovis. War is a terrible thing, and a terrible risk. The long peace may have softened the hearts of your people, and your soldiers from want of practice may have lost the habit of working together on the battlefield. Ere yet blood is shed, draw back if possible. We are sending ambassadors to the King of the Franks to try to prevent this war between our relatives; and the ambassadors whom we are sending to you will go on to Gundobad, King of the Burgundians, to get him to interpose on behalf of peace. Your enemy will be mine also'.

Before the Ostrogoths could come to his aid Alaric was forced to give battle by his own men who were incensed that their king took no decisive action while their lands were being plundered. The battle fought at Vouilé, near Poitiers, determined the future of France but unfortunately we know very little about it. Theodoric's attempted alliance with the Burgundians did not materialize, instead they fought alongside the Franks. With the Visigoths spread over the vast area of southern France and much of Spain it is unlikely that Alaric could have called on every Gothic warrior in his kingdom while Clovis had all his followers to hand. This was why Alaric needed Theodoric's reinforcements. He was, however, able to call on some Romans to reinforce his ranks as Procopius describes:

'[After the dissolution of the West Roman Empire units of Roman soldiers] having no means of returning to Rome… gave themselves, together with their military standards and the land which they had long been guarding for the Romans, to the [Goths]; and they handed down to their offspring all the customs of their fathers, which were thus preserved… For even at the present day [mid sixth century] they are clearly recognized as belonging to the legions to which they were assigned when they served in ancient times, and they always carry their own standards when they enter battle, and always follow the customs of their fathers. And they preserve the dress of the Romans in every particular, even as regards their shoes'. (Procopius)

It was not enough. Alaric was defeated and killed at Vouilé. Clovis overran most of the Visigothic Gallic territories, captured Toulouse and even reached Barcelona. Procopius tells us they captured the royal treasure 'which Alaric the elder in earlier times had taken as booty when he captured Rome. Among these were also the treasures of Solomon, King of the Hebrews, a most noteworthy sight. For the most of them were adorned with emeralds; and they had been taken from Jerusalem by the Romans in ancient times'.

Theodoric the Ostrogoth's letter to Alaric II indicates that he believed the martial abilities of the Visigoths had slipped since the glory days of the first Alaric, Wallia and the Visigothic Theodoric. Maybe it was because they were spread too thinly or that their 'soldiers from want of practice may have lost the habit of working together on the battlefield' to use the Ostrogothic King's own words. The victories won by their ancestors when they were moving together as a cohesive group through the Balkans, Italy, France and Spain were a thing of the past. Up against Clovis' aggressive Franks the Visigoths experienced only defeat.

Clovis was stopped by the intervention of the Ostrogoths who drove the Franks out of the coastal strip between the lower Rhone and the Pyrenees but the Visigothic heartland of Aquitaine was lost forever. From this point onwards Spain would become the Kingdom of the Visigoths while Italy was the heart of the Ostrogothic Kingdom.

Theodoric the Ostrogoth did away with Gesalic, Alaric's illegitimate son whom the surviving Visigoths had proclaimed king. In his stead he appointed his own daughter's child, Amalaric, with himself as regent. 'He [Theodoric] continued to send commanders and armies into Gaul and Spain, thus holding the real power of the government himself, and by way of providing that he should hold it securely and permanently, he ordained that the rulers of those countries should bring tribute to him. And though he received this every year, in order not to give the appearance of being greedy for money he sent it as an annual gift to the army of the Ostrogoths and Visigoths. And as a result of this, the Ostrogoths and Visigoths, as time went on, ruled as they were by one man and holding the same land, betrothed their children to one another and thus joined the two races in kinship'. (Procopius)

The Ostrogothic intervention and retrenchment in Spain gave the Visigoths a breathing space but conflict with the Franks continued. In 531 Amalaric was defeated by the Franks near Barcelona. Some contemporary accounts claim he was murdered by his own men while others say he died at the hands of the Franks. Either way, Amalaric's death brought about the end of the dynasty which had been founded by the first Alaric.

The Visigoths elected Theudis as their next king. He was actually an Ostrogoth who was previously a leader of Theodoric's household troops and had remained in Spain to support Amalaric. Theudis succeeded in holding back Frankish expansion, defeating an invading army in a battle of which we unfortunately have no detail. It was during his reign that the East Romans under Belisarius and Solomon destroyed the Vandal Kingdom in North Africa. The Romans also took Ceuta, a Visigothic enclave near modern Tangiers. A Visigothic expedition to re-take it ended in disaster and in 548 Theudis was murdered. This brought to a close the period of Ostrogothic involvement in Visigothic affairs as by this time, as we shall see, they had more pressing problems to deal with closer to home.

Before returning to the affairs of the Ostrogoths in Italy it is worth picking up on a few aspects of the Visigothic Kingdom. The beginning of a royal dynasty had begun to emerge amongst the successors of Alaric I but this royal family died out with Amalaric. Thereafter the powerful nobles who formed the King's household troops elected one of their own to the throne. In many ways this was closer to the Roman tradition of troops proclaiming an emperor than later medieval practice. The other point of note is how the Visigoths integrated their Roman subjects. We have previously seen how closely the Gallo-Roman aristocrats cooperated with the Visigoths in the early years and how Roman troops served alongside them. Theudis took a Hispano-Roman wife. '[She] belonged to the house of one of the wealthy inhabitants of that land, and not only possessed great wealth but also owned a large estate in Spain. From this estate he [Theudis] gathered about 2,000 soldiers and surrounded himself with a force of bodyguards'. (Procopius)

As far as we can tell the Visigoths ruled Spain with a thinly spread elite and a royal household which eventually concentrated at Toledo. Much of the power rested with the regional nobility, some of whom were of Roman origin. Although full integration of Goths and Romans was hindered by religious differences and various legal prohibitions, intermarriage may well have been quite common, such as that between Theudis and his Roman wife. In this way the Visigoth and Roman elites began to merge and share power.

Theodoric the Great

When Theodoric led the Ostrogoths into Italy the fiction that many Romans held to was that he was leading an army in Constantinople's service to liberate Italy from Odoacer and bring the country back into the Imperial fold. For much of the fifth century Constantinople was the true source of Roman power and the various short-lived Western emperors had to have Constantinople's blessing to have any legitimacy. As we saw in the previous chapter, Theodoric did not step aside to allow Constantinople to appoint a new Western Emperor. For most Italians this did not matter. Most of those who cared about such things still considered Italy to be the Western Roman Empire. Roman law remained in effect, the machinery of imperial government was intact, the Senate continued to meet, and ancient offices were still held by aristocratic Romans.

Many Italians saw Theodoric not as an invading barbarian but almost as a new West Roman Emperor in all but name. They hailed him as a second Trajan — someone who could invigorate Italy and restore past glories. With the benefit of his upbringing as a hostage at Constantinople, Theodoric knew how to look and act the part and could relate to the Romans on their terms. With a strong army at his back he brought western Illyricum back under Italian control — something even

Stilicho had failed to achieve. When southern Gaul was threatened by the Franks he intervened to stabilize the situation. He brought the coastal strip of Provence under his authority and exercised sovereignty over the Visigoths in Spain.

Theodoric's support of the Visigoths against the Franks could be viewed as little more than one branch of Goths propping up the other. To most Romans, however, it would have seemed like the sort of actions an effective emperor was expected to take. Theodoric could be seen to be intervening against an external threat to restore the *Res Publica* of Rome. By appointing himself as regent over an infant Visigothic king he was following in the footsteps of Stilicho and many other Roman warlords of the fifth century.

Theodoric's Goths were not just defending the Roman way of life but actually living it. Theodoric is quoted as saying that the noble Goth should imitate the Roman: 'You may display the justice of the Goths. They have always maintained a praiseworthy means, since they have acquired the wisdom of the Romans and have inherited the uprightness of the tribes'. (Cassiodorus). The Ostrogoths probably did more to preserve Rome than destroy her. Despite the popular image of barbaric savages rampaging through the cities and destroying ancient monuments there is plenty of evidence to show that the opposite was true. In a letter to the Senate of Rome, Theodoric shows his concern with the destruction of public buildings:

'Our care is for the whole Republic, in which, by the favour of God, we are striving to bring back all things to their former state; but especially for the City of Rome. We hear that great depredations are being committed on public property there... Great weights of brass and lead (the latter very easy to steal, from its softness) have been stripped off from the public buildings... Temples and other public buildings, which at the request of many we assigned for repair, have instead been given over to demolition... We have appointed the distinguished John to inquire into and set straight all these matters... Now give your attention, apply your care, so that you may be seen to carry out with readiness and inquiry that you ought to have requested'. (Cassiodorus)

The Ostrogoths in Italy were settled amongst the Romans according to the system developed in the fifth century whereby landowners were expected to give up a third of their holdings — either in actual land or equivalent tax revenue — to support the Imperial armies. The Ostrogoths took over the possessions of some of Odoacer's followers but Theodoric chose to incorporate many of Odoacer's men into his kingdom rather than dispossess them all. This left him the tricky problem of finding ways to give his men the land they were seeking without destroying the productivity of the Roman estates. Writing in the early years of the sixth century

Cassiodorus reminded his fellow senators of the benefits of sharing in a wonderful example of ancient 'spin':

> 'We especially like to remember how in the assignment of the Thirds he [Theodoric] joined both the possessions and the hearts of the Goths and Romans alike... The friendship of the lords has been joined with the division of the soil. Amity has grown out of the loss of the provincials and by the land a defender [Theodoric] has been gained whose occupation of part guarantees the quiet enjoyment of the whole'.

Land redistribution is never an easy thing to accomplish. Even in modern times we have plenty of examples of the disastrous consequences that can follow. Robert Mugabe's redistribution of formerly prosperous Rhodesian farms to his 'war veterans' transformed Zimbabwe from a food exporting nation into one which had to rely on expensive imports to feed its people. Somehow Theodoric managed to avoid this. He settled his Goths in lands around Pavia, Ravenna and Picenum in the north of Italy. There were too few of them to spread all over the country as he needed to have his warriors close at hand in case he had to call on them. This is not to say that everything went smoothly. The courts were kept busy sorting out disputes and appeals over various land claims for many years. This goes to show that Theodoric took care to keep the Roman nobility on side and not act like a conqueror. This is in marked contrast to the Vandals in Africa who simply appropriated all the good estates for themselves.

In Gaul and Spain the Visigoths drew on the native Romans to serve in their armies but while the Gallic provincials had some recent history of military service it had been centuries since many native Italians had served in a Roman army. Theodoric, therefore, had to rely primarily on the men he had led into Italy along with those remnants of Odoacer's followers who had not been purged. In the fifth century local forces were raised in Italy so it is possible that some city garrisons included Romans as well as Goths. During the siege of Naples in 536 Jewish citizens fought alongside the Goths although these were probably volunteers rather than soldiers.

Away from his northern Italian heartland Theodoric established garrisons in key areas throughout Italy, Sicily and in the frontier regions of Provence and Illyricum. There are some indications that in Illyricum the Ostrogoths may have absorbed existing Roman garrisons into their army as well as training and arming provincials. In those areas of northern Italy where the Goths were concentrated, many of them became farmers while the elites remained professional soldiers who might either man the far-flung garrisons or form the core of Theodoric's household troops.

Although some historians have portrayed it as such, it would be too simple to see Theodoric's reign as a period where Romans and Goths lived in complete harmony. There were constant tensions and Theodoric had to walk a tight rope to keep everything in balance. Yet he managed it, not only keeping Constantinople at bay but also allying himself with the most important barbarian successor kingdoms of the Western Empire. We have already seen how Theodoric took the Visigoths under his wing through a combination of family alliances and military intervention. He married Audefleda, daughter of the Frankish king Childeric. He gave his sister Amalafrida to the Vandal king Thrasamund and one of his daughters to the Burgundian king Sigismund.

In the early 520s it looked as if Theodoric had managed to fuse Goths and Romans to create a new stable society from the ashes of the West Roman Empire. The prospects for the future looked good. The Western Empire had not been re-established but a reasonable facsimile operated in Italy and its influence was spreading beyond its borders. In 519 Theodoric's son-in-law Eutharic even shared the consulship with the East Roman Emperor Justin.

> 'In governing his own subjects, he [Theodoric] invested himself with all the qualities which appropriately belong to one who is by birth an emperor. For he was exceedingly careful to observe justice, he preserved the laws on a sure basis, he protected the land and kept it safe from the barbarians dwelling round about, and attained the highest possible degree of wisdom and manliness. And he himself committed scarcely a single act of injustice against his subjects, nor would he brook such conduct on the part of anyone else who attempted it, except, indeed, that the Goths distributed among themselves the portion of the lands which Odoacer had given to his own partisans. And although in name Theodoric was a usurper, yet in fact he was as truly an emperor as any who have distinguished themselves in this office from the beginning; and love for him among both Goths and Italians grew to be great… Theodoric reigned for thirty-seven years, and when he died, he had not only made himself an object of terror to all his enemies, but he also left to his subjects a keen sense of bereavement at his loss'. (Procopius)

Even before Theodoric's death, his dream of a new Romano-Gothic society had begun to unravel. Religious disputes and bickering amongst the Roman senatorial class as they jockeyed for power and influence made it increasingly difficult for Theodoric to maintain a consensus. An increasing number of Roman aristocrats looked to forge closer links with Constantinople while many of the Gothic nobles were drawn into factional politics. There are also some indications that an increasing gulf was opening up between the Gothic nobles and their poorer followers. Amongst the former many saw the benefits of full integration with the top echelons of Roman society which was beyond the reach of many of their poorer followers.

To compound Theodoric's problems the various alliances he had forged with other barbarian kingdoms began to fall apart. The Frankish alliance was destroyed by their war with the Visigoths. When Amalafrida's Vandal husband died in 523 the Vandal nobles rose up in revolt against Hilderic his successor. Amalafrida became their champion and in the civil war that followed she was defeated and imprisoned. Even the Visigoths drifted away from the Ostrogoths. When Theudis became king he adopted an alarmingly independent stance even though he was an Ostrogoth himself.

Theodoric died in 526, to be succeeded by his 8-year-old grandson Athalaric with his mother Amalasuntha as regent (Eutharic, his father having pre-deceased him). The following year Justinian became East Roman Emperor in Constantinople and the shifting political plates set in motion a series of events which would change the course of history once again.

Chapter 9

The Road to War

Gothic Power Struggle

We should not be surprised to learn that with a minor ruling them the Ostrogothic nobility split apart into various factions. Amalasuntha did her best to continue her late father's policy of uniting Romans and Goths but if this had become increasingly difficult for the great Theodoric, it was much harder for his daughter. Although it is probably a bit too simplistic, the Goths split into two main factions. Led by Amalasuintha, some favoured continuing integration and cooperation with the Roman nobility and the court at Constantinople. Others were more hostile to the Empire and sought to instill the manly ways of the Gothic warrior in their child king to combat the pro-Roman influences of his mother. This conflict is summed up by Procopius:

'Now Amalasuntha wished to make her son resemble the Roman princes in his manner of life, and was already compelling him to attend the school of a teacher of letters. And she chose three old men of the Goths whom she knew to be prudent and refined above all the others, and bade them live with Athalaric. But the Goths were by no means pleased with this... They wished to be ruled by him more after the barbarian fashion. On one occasion the mother, finding the boy doing some wrong in his chamber, chastised him; and he in tears went off thence to the men's apartments. And some Goths who met him made a great to-do about this, and reviling Amalasuntha insisted that she wished to put the boy out of the world as quickly as possible, in order that she might marry a second husband and with him rule over the Goths and Italians. And all the notable men among them gathered together, and coming before Amalasuntha made the charge that their king was not being educated correctly... For letters, they said, are far removed from manliness, and the teaching of old men results for the most part in a cowardly and submissive spirit... They added that even Theodoric would never allow any of the Goths to send their children to school; for he used to say to them all that, if the fear of the strap once came over them, they would never have the resolution to despise sword or spear'.

With many of the Gothic nobles against her, Amalasuntha turned to the new East Roman Emperor Justinian for support and even made plans to flee to Constantinople. Athalaric's reign did not last long. When her son died of disease in 534, Amalasuntha supported her cousin Theodahad to succeed him. According to Procopius, Theodahad was: 'A man already of mature years, versed in Latin literature and the teachings of Plato, but without any experience whatever in war and taking no part in active life, and yet extraordinarily devoted to the pursuit of money'. On the surface Theodahad was a supporter of Theodoric's legacy which Amalasuntha was trying to maintain. In reality he was completely self-serving.

When Theodahad became king he imprisoned Amalasuntha. He then set about to win the support of those Gothic nobles she had alienated and then had her killed. This did not go down well in Constantinople as the Emperor Justinian had seen Amalasuntha as a pro-Roman ally while Theodahad was rallying the anti-Roman Gothic faction to his cause. As Procopius reports, 'When the Emperor Justinian heard these things, he formed the purpose of throwing the Goths and Theodahad into confusion... [the Emperor's envoy] protested openly to Theodahad and the other Goths that because this base deed [Amalasuntha's murder] had been committed by them, there would be war without truce between the Emperor and themselves'.

Before recounting the events of the war which brought about the end of the Ostrogothic Kingdom we need to turn briefly to what was happening in the East Roman Empire at the time of Theodoric's death and the power struggles amongst the Gothic nobles.

Justinian Looks West

Justinian ascended to the throne in 527, the year after Theodoric's death. He was young, energetic and in the first years of his reign he concluded a reasonably successful war against the Persians. By 533 the East Roman Empire's frontiers were secure, riots in Constantinople had been suppressed and the Roman army was led by the rising star of Belisarius, who had won victory against the Persians and put down the riots with a brutal efficiency. Greek was replacing Latin as the principal language of the Eastern Empire but Justinian was a native Latin speaker who looked to the West and dreamed of re-establishing Rome's ancient glories.

Constantinople had never formally approved Theodoric's rule over Italy but the court had been more or less content to leave things as they were, especially as Theodoric was careful to preserve Roman law and maintain good relations with the eastern half of the Empire. The Gothic power struggles which followed Theodoric's death began to change things in the latter half of the 520s and early 530s. It was growing abundantly clear that good relations were breaking down but before turning his attention to Ostrogothic Italy, Justinian had a higher priority.

In 533 he sent his general Belisarius to re-conquer Africa from the Vandals, the full story of which is told in the previous book in this series. With only 16,000 men Belisarius defeated the Vandal king Gelimer and re-established Roman control over North Africa. One of the keys to his success was Amalasuntha's support in allowing the Romans access to Sicily. Only a day's sail away from the African coast it was the perfect safe harbour and supply base. All previous Roman expeditions against the Vandals had used Sicily as their jumping off place but then Sicily had been under Roman control. Now it was part of the Ostrogothic Kingdom of Italy. Amalasuntha was not best pleased with the Vandals in the aftermath of her aunt Amalafrida's execution by Hilderic. When Justinian's envoys approached her, she was more than happy to provide a supply base in Sicily for a Roman force which would avenge Amalafrida's death.

In the mopping up operations which followed their victory over the Vandals in 534, some Roman troops went to Sicily to take over the port town of Lilybaeum. This had been given to the Vandals by Theodoric as part of his sister Amalafrida's dowry when she married the Vandal king Thrasamund. As it had been part of the Vandal Kingdom Belisarius believed it should now be part of the spoils of victory. This was the same year in which Athalaric died and the various Gothic factions were manoeuvring to fill the power vacuum. The local Gothic commander in Sicily occupied Lilybaeum before the Romans could land. Whether he did this on his own initiative or under Amalasuntha's instructions we will never know. Seeing a Gothic garrison in place with no intention of handing Lilybaeum over to him Belisarius backed down and referred the matter to Constantinople for Justinian's decision.

Procopius reports that Justinian sent a letter of protest to the Ostrogoths. 'The fortress of Lilybaeum, which is ours, you have taken by force and are now holding, and barbarians, slaves of mine who have run away, you have received and have not even yet decided to restore them to me'.

Amalasuntha's response was to remind Justinian of the support she had given him: 'You threaten Athalaric on account of Lilybaeum, and ten runaways, and a mistake made by soldiers in going against their enemies, which through some mis-apprehension chanced to affect a friendly city. Do not do this, oh Emperor, but call to mind that when you were making war upon the Vandals, we not only refrained from hindering you, but quite zealously even gave you free passage against the enemy and provided a market in which to buy the indispensable supplies, fur-nishing especially the multitude of horses to which your final mastery over the enemy was chiefly due... And consider that at that time your fleet had no other place at which to put in from the sea except Sicily, and that without the supplies bought there it could not go on to Libya. Therefore you are indebted to us for the chief cause of your victory... And yet in our case the outcome is that we suffer no slight disadvantage, in that we do not, in accordance with the custom of war, enjoy our share of the spoils. And now you are also claiming the right to despoil us of Lilybaeum in Sicily, which has belonged to the Goths from ancient times'.

According to Procopius this message was written openly by Amalasuntha, implying that she did so to appease those Gothic nobles who wanted to take a strong stance against the Empire. He adds that she wrote a secret message to Justinian in which she agreed to 'put the whole of Italy into his hands', no doubt to escape the enemies who were closing in on her. Theodahad owned extensive estates in Tuscany and before he became king he had opened negotiations with Justinian to hand them over to the Empire in exchange for a large sum of money and asylum in Constantinople. As he and Amalasuntha became locked in a power struggle, both sought Justinian's support.

No doubt Justinian had already set his sight on Italy as well as Africa. Buoyed up by the initial success of the African expedition (even though conflict continued for many more years) and given the opportunity of the Gothic power struggle, he used Amalasuntha's murder as the excuse to intervene.

The Empire Closes In

Justinian planned a two-pronged attack on the Ostrogoths. In 535 he ordered Mundo, the commander of Roman forces in Illyricum to advance into Dalmatia which was under Gothic control. At the same time he sent Belisarius by sea to invade Sicily with 4000 regular soldiers and *foederati*, 3000 Isaurians, 300 Moors and 200 Huns. Belisarius' instructions were to let it be known that his destination was Carthage, but on landing in Sicily he was to bring the island under his control. If he ran into difficulty he should withdraw to Carthage. Justinian also sent envoys with pockets full of cash to the Franks, encouraging them to join in an alliance and invade Italy from the northwest.

This seems like an impossibly small force with which to contemplate the re-conquest of Italy. Given Belisarius' orders it may have been that at this stage Justinian simply wanted to probe the Gothic resolve. If Belisarius could take Sicily with 7,500 men then that would be a great accomplishment. If he failed he could withdraw by sea to Carthage and Justinian would have to think again. We have already seen in Chapter 7 that Theodoric Strabo had 13,000 warriors and that the force Theodoric the Great led into Italy was probably something in the region of 20,000 men. Probably he added a few more after incorporating Odoacer's followers but the dispersed garrisons from Sicily through to Provence and Dalmatia could not have been very strong. Furthermore they would not have had larger forces close at hand to intervene on their behalf as the only large concentration of Gothic warriors was around Ravenna and Pavia in northeastern Italy. Belisarius had succeeded in wresting Africa from the Vandals with only 16,000 men. Of these only the 6000 cavalry ever really saw any real action. The 10,000 Roman infantry served to hold ground, guard the baggage and garrison captured towns. The prospect of taking thinly garrisoned Sicily with 7,500 men may, therefore, not have seemed such an impossible task.

The opening moves went badly for the Ostrogoths. Mundo defeated a Gothic army in Dalmatia and captured Salona (near Split in modern Croatia). When Belisarius landed in Sicily, Catania, Syracuse other most other cities surrendered without a fight. Only the port city of Panormus (modern Palermo) offered any resistance but it too gave up when Belisarius sent archers up the masts of his ships from where they could shoot down over the parapets of the walled city. The Sicilians welcomed Belisarius as a liberator. When he marched into Syracuse he was 'loudly applauded by the army and by the Sicilians'. (Procopius) Sicily was a vital base for the East Romans. It made their hold on Africa more secure and gave them a jumping off place for any intervention into Italy. The mountainous approaches into Italy from the northeast were much harder to force and it was there that the Ostrogoths were concentrated in large numbers.

Justinian then turned the diplomatic screws on Theodahad. He hoped to get him to agree to retire to Constantinople and place the Ostrogoths under Imperial authority as *foederati* rather than independent rulers of Italy. The loss of Sicily and Imperial control of North Africa closed off vital food supplies for the Goths. For years Italy had depended on grain shipments from North Africa to feed its population — especially the city of Rome. When these were cut off, first by the Vandals and then by the East Romans, Sicily had become increasingly important. Now with hostile Franks to the northwest and Constantinople extending its control to the northeast and south, Italy was cut off and surrounded. Holding onto power looked increasingly difficult for Theodahad, especially given the dubious circumstances which had brought him to the throne.

Any possibility of a deal was scuppered when Asinarius and Gripas, two Gothic leaders in Dalmatia, counter-attacked Mundo's troops in Dalmatia.

'When they had reached the neighbourhood of Salona, Mauricius, the son of Mundo, who was not marching out for battle but, with a few men, was on a scouting expedition, encountered them. A violent engagement ensued in which the Goths lost their foremost and noblest men, but the Romans almost their whole company, including their general Mauricius. And when Mundus heard of this, being overcome with grief at the misfortune and by this time dominated by a mighty fury, he went against the enemy without the least delay and regardless of order. The battle which took place was stubbornly contested, and the result was a [Pyrrhic] victory for the Romans. For although the most of the enemy fell and their rout had been decisive, Mundus went on killing and following up the enemy wherever he chanced to find them and was quite unable to restrain his mind because of the misfortune of his son. He was wounded by some fugitive or other and fell. Thereupon the pursuit ended and the two armies separated'. (Procopius)

Mundo withdrew from Dalmatia and the Goths re-took Salona whose inhabitants were friendly to them. 'But when the Emperor Justinian heard these things and what had taken place in Dalmatia, he sent Constantinus... into Illyricum, bidding him gather an army from there and make an attempt on Salona, in whatever manner he might be able; and he commanded Belisarius to enter Italy with all speed and to treat the Goths as enemies'. (Procopius) Any hope of a negotiated settlement had been dashed. Total war followed which would wipe out the Ostrogothic Kingdom and devastate Italy.

The Roman Army

The Roman army had changed radically from that which had faced the Goths at Adrianople more than 150 years earlier. The familiar legions and auxiliaries who had formed the main strength of previous Roman armies were now relegated to a supporting role. When Belisarius took Africa from the Vandals, infantry still formed the bulk of his army but they never took offensive action. The main strength of the East Roman army now lay in its cavalry. Most of these were mounted archers but they were not lightly equipped skirmishers. Wearing body armour of mail or scale and equipped with good swords they were perfectly happy closing into hand to hand combat as well as shooting arrows from a distance. Some also carried spears in addition to their bows and swords but probably not all of them. This transformation of the regular Roman cavalry into horse archers probably came about gradually during the fifth century under the influence of the Huns and Persians.

Procopius describes the Roman cavalry of his day:

'The bowmen of the present time go into battle wearing corselets and fitted out with greaves [leg protectors] which extend up to the knee. From the right hand side hang their arrows, from the other a sword. And there are those who have a spear also attached to them, and at the shoulders a sort of small shield without a grip, such as to cover the region of the face and neck. They are expert horsemen and are able without difficulty to direct their bows to either side while riding at full speed, and to shoot at an opponent whether in pursuit or flight. They draw the bowstring along by the forehead about opposite the right ear, thereby discharging the arrow with such an impetus as to kill whoever stands in the way shield and corselet alike having no power to check its force'.

The later sixth century military manual, the *Strategikon*, describes the training exercises carried out by the Roman cavalryman of the time to enable him to use both missile and shock tactics:

'On horseback at a run, he should fire one or two arrows rapidly and put the strung bow in its case. Then he should grab the spear which he has been carrying on his back. With the strung bow in its case, he should hold the spear in his hand, then quickly replace it on his back and grab the bow'.

This made the Roman cavalryman of the mid sixth century someone who could either fight from a distance or close into combat. He could ride up to his opponents, shower them with arrows, retreat out of harms way and then suddenly turn back to attack with spear or sword. These regular Roman troopers were augmented by a number of foreign auxiliaries. These included fast moving lightly equipped Moorish cavalry armed with javelins and Hun horse archers. 3,000 Isaurians provided auxiliary infantry when Belisarius landed in Sicily. These were tough men from the hills and mountains of Anatolia who operated in loose formations lightly equipped with javelins and shields. Later in the war other auxiliaries supplemented the regular Roman troops. These included Gepids, Lombards and Heruls. These Germanic warriors usually fought as cavalry but on several occasions they dismounted to fight on foot.

Amongst the regular Roman cavalry were the *foederati*. Initially this term described barbarians in Roman service but by the mid-fifth century it had come to mean something else. 'Now at an earlier time only the barbarians had been enlisted amongst the *foederati* ... but at the present time there is nothing to prevent anyone from assuming the name, since time will by no means consent to keep names attached to the things to which they were formerly applied'. (Procopius)

Just as a man serving in a regiment of light cavalry in today's British army is neither necessarily light nor a horseman, a trooper in a regiment of *foederati* in the sixth century Roman army was not necessarily a barbarian in the way that a fourth or fifth century Roman would have understood the term. It may be that the *foederati* were spear and shield armed cavalry of the same type as the majority of the Goths in contrast to the bow-armed Romans and Huns.

Belisarius and the other Roman generals were also accompanied by their own household troops known as *bucellarii*. These men are referred to variously as *doruphoroi* (spear bearers) and *hypapsistai* (shield bearers). The former appear to have been a sort of inner guard who also acted as staff officers while the latter were elite cavalrymen. All were probably very well equipped mounted warriors with body armour, bows, spears, swords and shields. They owed their loyalty to the general personally and were maintained by him rather than by the state.

The role of the regular Roman infantry was to hold ground, provide a secure rallying point for the cavalry, guard the baggage and garrison any towns captured along the way. They were typically a mix of spearmen and archers with the former deployed in the front ranks forming a phalanx and protected by large oval shields, with the latter shooting overhead from behind. Typically the archers accounted for about a quarter of the infantry.

The Ostrogothic Army

The men that Theodoric led into Italy at the end of the fifth century were probably all warriors in one way or another. With no land to call their own they had to fight either to take what they needed or to honour their agreements with their Roman paymasters. Yet even then there were clear divisions between a warrior elite and their lesser followers. When their ancestors were living under Hun overlordship many would have been primarily farmers, providing essential food supplies for the Huns while the elites served in Attila's army. When they settled in Italy this again became the norm. The poorer Goths probably became farmers although they retained a military obligation. The elites took on the trappings of the Roman aristocracy, ran large estates, commanded the King's armies and surrounded themselves with paid retainers.

The elite warriors and their retainers fought on horseback. Unlike the fifth century Visigoths and their earlier ancestors, the sixth century Ostrogoths seemed less inclined to dismount to fight on foot although they did so on a number of occasions. In Chapter 7 we saw how some of the Ostrogoths in Attila's army may have been influenced by the Sarmatians and adopted the two-handed lance. Perhaps some Ostrogothic nobles used a long two-handed lance without a shield while others used the more conventional combination of spear and shield supplemented by javelins.

However they were armed, the Ostrogothic cavalry preferred hand-to-hand combat and their charge could be devastating. Their problem was that they did not really have any response to the skirmish tactics of the Romans. According to Procopius, when Belisarius was asked how he had managed to defeat the Ostrogoths with such small numbers: 'He said that in engaging with them at the first with only a few men he had noticed just what the difference was between the two armies... And the difference was that practically all the Romans and their allies, the Huns, are good mounted bowmen, but not a man among the Goths has had practice in this branch, for their horsemen are accustomed to use only spears and swords, while their bowmen enter battle on foot and under cover of the heavy-armed men. So the horsemen, unless the engagement is at close quarters, have no means of defending themselves against opponents who use the bow, and therefore can easily be reached by the arrows and destroyed; and as for the foot-soldiers, they can never be strong enough to make sallies against men on horseback'.

So the Ostrogothic nobles and their retainers formed the mounted offensive arm whose main tactic was to charge the enemy line. The poorer classes provided a combination of foot archers protected by spear and shield armed men. Some modern historians have concluded that the foot warriors were all archers but this seems highly unlikely. Procopius (quoted above) is quite specific about the archers being protected by 'heavy armed men' and here are several other battle descriptions which indicate that the Gothic foot included 'some with spears and some with bows'. It is reasonable to assume that the spearmen usually carried standard Germanic and late Roman round or oval shields but there are tantalizing hints that larger mantlets may also have been used. Procopius mentions these at the siege of Rome. As [the Goths] advanced 'they held before them shields no smaller than the long shields used by the Persians'. Whether these mantlets were a one-off for a siege operation or something used more often is anyone's guess.

Theoretically this combination of foot archers protected by spearmen along with a strike force of heavy cavalry should have enabled the Ostrogoths to deal with the skirmish tactics of the bow-armed Roman cavalry. Foot archers could outrange and outshoot horse archers. If they were drawn up behind a line of men with spears and large shields then the Roman cavalry would not have been able to close with them. In close combat the Ostrogothic cavalry were more than a match for the Romans and they could have used their infantry as strong points on the battlefield to charge out from and rally behind if things went badly.

This required close cooperation between horse and foot to succeed and it called for much more sophisticated tactics than the Goths usually managed to achieve. The Ostrogothic elite trained for war on a regular basis as the letters of Cassiodorus show. Apart from managing their estates warfare was their only real occupation — much like the medieval knights who came after them. The men who filled the ranks of the Ostrogothic foot were not full time soldiers and, in contrast to the Romans, the various divisions of the Gothic army do not seem to have trained together to develop the sort of tactics which enabled horse and foot to operate on the battlefield as a cohesive whole.

There were times when the combination of Gothic heavy cavalry supported by mixed foot archers and spearmen did achieve the desired result. Describing the action in a battle outside Rome Procopius tells us that the Gothic cavalry were driven back by Belisarius' Romans. '[Meanwhile] the rest of the barbarian army stayed very near their camps and, protecting themselves with their shields, vigorously warded off their opponents, destroying many men and a much larger number of horses... Finally the horsemen of the barbarians who were on the right wing, taking note of this, advanced at a gallop against the enemy opposite them'.

This was probably good luck rather than good management as more often than not the Ostrogothic leaders put all their faith in their cavalry and more or less ignored the infantry. At the Battle of Taginae in 552 the Goths put all their cavalry in the first line with the infantry behind them. This gave no opportunity for the Gothic foot to support the horsemen and when the latter were defeated the infantry were simply caught up in the rout.

Although the Ostrogoths were perhaps lacking in tactical finesse, theirs was not an army of ill-disciplined half-naked barbarian savages. It was an army which had perhaps done more than many fifth century West Roman armies to restore Italy's prestige and influence. It was paid for, supplied and equipped by the state which had full access to the armouries of Italy and all the wealth the country could provide. The men who filled its ranks would have had as good equipment as any of the East Romans opposing them. In appearance and custom they were as much a 'Roman' army as that sent from Constantinople. Perhaps more so considering that the Greek speaking East Roman officers commanded troops of Armenian, Isaurian, Persian, Germanic and Hun origins.

Procopius even claims that the Ostrogothic elite cavalry had horse armour. In describing the army which the Goths marshalled for a counter-attack against Belisarius he says that they had 'not less than 150,000 men, and the most of them as well as their horses were clad in armour'.

The numbers alone would lead us to conclude that this is nothing other than exaggerated propaganda on Procopius' part. Unless the Goths had conscripted the Italian peasantry of northern Italy — which they certainly did not — then it is hard to imagine how they could have mustered much over 20–30,000 men given the numbers that had followed Theodoric into Italy at the end of the fifth century. Therefore most historians have also dismissed any claim that any, let alone 'most horses were clad in armour'.

Let us pause for a moment on the matter of horse armour. It is perfectly reasonable to assume that the ancestors of the sixth century Ostrogoths had been influenced by the Sarmatians in their early days beyond the Danube and maybe incorporated some of them when they crossed into Roman territory. The Sarmatians were famed for their heavily armoured cavalry, many of whom also rode armoured horses as depicted on Trajan's column. The Romans themselves raised units of *cataphractarii* (very heavy armoured cavalry) modelled on the Sarmatians and probably initially raised from Sarmatian prisoners of war. Although we must reject

Procopius' claim that the Ostrogoths could muster 150,000 men, do we also have to reject his assertion that some Goths had armoured horses?

The Sarmatians were notoriously poor and the Ostrogoths infamously rich. Yet there is little doubt that some Sarmatian nobles rode armoured horses. Is it unreasonable to believe that some of the Ostrogothic nobility with all the wealth of Italy at their disposal would not have decided to kit out their horses with armour? They had not only the Sarmatian influence to draw from, as they would have been more than familiar with the units of *catafractarii* in the Roman army. I am, therefore, not inclined to reject Procopius' assertion of horse armour out of hand. I believe it is highly possible that some of the richer Ostrogoths would have ridden armoured horses even if I do not think that the majority of them did, nor that they had specialized units of *catafractarii*.

Chapter 10

The War for Italy

The long bitter struggle between Ostrogoths and Romans from 536 to 555 is worthy of a book in its own right. Unlike the sparsely documented years of the Gothic movements in the fifth century we have Procopius' more or less firsthand account to describe the intimate details of the politics, battles and sieges which brought about the end of the Ostrogothic Kingdom of Italy.

The reign of Theodoric the Great brought a brief hope of a resurgent West Roman state under a benevolent dictatorship which might merge the best of Germanic and Roman cultures to restore a new equilibrium. The Gothic power struggle which followed his death and the two decades of war with the Eastern half of the Roman Empire destroyed this utterly and laid the foundations of medieval Europe.

Returning to where we left the narrative of events in the previous chapter, in late 536 Constantinus, aided by the Roman fleet, retook Salona and 'gained possession of all Dalmatia and Liburnia, bringing over to his side all the Goths who were settled there'. (Procopius). Early in 536 Belisarius invaded Italy and marched on Naples. He met little or no resistance. As Procopius recounts: 'Every day the people of that region kept coming over to him. For since their towns had from of old been without walls, they had no means at all of guarding them, and because of their hostility toward the Goths they were, as was natural, greatly dissatisfied with their present government. And Ebrimous came over to Belisarius as a deserter from the Goths, together with all his followers'.

Naples was garrisoned and for a while held out, the local Jewish population bolstering the Gothic defenders who had protected them from Catholic persecution. The city fell after Belisarius' men found a route through an aqueduct and a bloody massacre ensued. Apart from Naples there was little resistance and Belisarius moved further up the Italian peninsular, his fleet following up off-shore to support the land forces.

A Germanic king's authority rested in the belief of his people that he would protect them and share with them the spoils of victory. Theodahad, whose position was tenuous at best, apparently did nothing to stop Belisarius' advance. 'Theodahad was not making the least preparation for war, being by nature unmanly... The Goths who were at Rome and in the country round about had even before [the fall of Naples] regarded with great amazement his inactivity, because, though the enemy was in his neighbourhood, he was unwilling to engage them in battle, and they felt among themselves much suspicion toward him, believing that he was betraying the cause of the Goths to the Emperor Justinian of his own free will, and cared for nothing else than that he himself might live in quiet, possessed of as much money as possible'.

The Gothic nobles deposed Theodahad and killed him. Then they elected Witiges as their new king. 'After this he [Witiges] began to gather all the Goths from every side and to organize and equip them, duly distributing arms and horses to each one. Only the Goths who were engaged in garrison duty in Gaul he was unable to summon, through fear of the Franks'.

Witiges sent 4000 men to garrison Rome but the city fell when the Gothic garrison realized they could not defend the extensive walls without the support of the populace which was not forthcoming. 'Rome became subject to the Romans again after a space of sixty years'. (Procopius)

Belisarius consolidated his hold on Rome and sent troops into Tuscany led by Bessas who himself was a Goth by birth but one of those who had remained in Thrace rather than following Theodoric into Italy. Welcomed by the local inhabitants Bessas had no trouble re-establishing Imperial control over Tuscany. In this he was aided by Constantinus who seems to have moved by sea from the Dalmatian coast to northern Italy (see Map 9).

> 'Now when Witiges heard this, he was no longer willing to remain quietly in Ravenna… So he sent to Dalmatia a great army with Asinarius and Uligisalus as its commanders, in order to recover Dalmatia for the Gothic rule. And he directed them to add to their own troops an army from the land of the Suevi, composed of the barbarians there, and then to proceed directly to Dalmatia and Salona. And he also sent with them many ships of war, in order that they might be able to besiege Salona both by land and by sea. But he himself was hastening to go with his whole army against Belisarius and Rome'. (Procopius)

The Siege of Rome

With a large army, certainly not the 150,000 quoted by Procopius, Witiges invested Rome. Maybe he had 20–30,000 men but it could hardly have been many more if the original strength of Theodoric's Goths had been close to that number when he came into Italy and Witiges had sent men into Dalmatia and had left others to hold Provence. Although Belisarius had been reinforced since his invasion of Sicily with 7,500 men, he was probably outnumbered by more than 2:1. Despite his numerical superiority, Witiges did not have enough men to surround Rome entirely. He built seven camps around the city and had to accept significant gaps in his lines.

After elaborate preparations Witiges attempted an assault with siege towers, scaling ladders and rams. The fighting was ferocious but eventually the Goths were driven off and their siege engines destroyed. So Witiges settled down to blockade the city even though he was unable to seal it completely.

When Alaric camped outside Rome more than a century earlier he was facing an undefended city and all he needed was to wait. The mere presence of his army was enough to potentially force terms and when this failed he was able to march into the city and sack it. With a strong garrison led by the brilliant general Belisarius, Witiges' task was much more difficult. He took the port of Pontus which meant that Rome would be starved of further re-supply by sea but it would be a while before the threat of starvation might induce surrender.

Belisarius led an active defence. He sent his light troops out to constantly harass the Goths and to tempt them into engagements in which he might be able to destroy the forces sent against him. A wonderful example of this is recorded by Procopius which helps to demonstrate the difference between the Roman and Gothic forces. Bolstered by 1,600 Hun reinforcements Belisarius decided to take the initiative.

'On the following day he commanded [his general Trajan] to take 200 horsemen of the guards and go straight towards the enemy, and as soon as they came near their camps to go up on a high hill and remain quietly there. If the enemy should come against them, he was not to allow the battle to come to close quarters, nor to touch sword or spear in any case, but to use bows only, and as soon as he should find that his quiver had no more arrows in it, he was to flee as hard as he could with no thought of shame and retire to the fortifications on the run.

'Having given these instructions, [Belisarius] held in readiness both the engines for shooting arrows and the men skilled in their use. Then Trajan with the 200 men went out from the Salarian Gate against the camp of the enemy. And they, being filled with amazement at the sudden-ness of the thing, rushed out from the camps, each man equipping him-self as well as he could. Trajan's men galloped to the top of the hill and from there began to ward off the barbarians with missiles. And since their shafts fell among a dense throng, they were for the most part successful in hitting a man or a horse. When all their missiles had at last failed them, they rode off to the rear with all speed, and the Goths kept pressing upon them in pursuit. When they came near the fortifications, the operators of the engines began to shoot arrows from them, and the barbarians became terrified and abandoned the pursuit. And it is said that not less than 1,000 Goths perished in this action'.

This small action wonderfully encapsulates the flexibility of the elite Roman horse archers, the difficulty the Goths had in coming to grips with them and the difficulty the Goths had in laying siege to a walled city defended by a determined enemy.

Their morale bolstered by this and similar actions, Belisarius' army and the citizens of Rome whom he had armed, demanded further offensive action against the Goths. Belisarius planned a two-pronged sortie. His main force would debouch from the Salarian and Pincian gates while a smaller force of Moorish cavalry and armed Roman citizens would come out to the Aurelian gate to stop the Goths from reinforcing those facing Belisarius' main effort.

In a telling example of how far the Roman infantry had fallen from the glory days of Caesar and Augustus, Procopius says that Belisarius wished:

> 'to engage in a cavalry battle only. Indeed most of the regular infantry were now unwilling to remain in their accustomed condition but since they had captured horses as booty from the enemy and had become not unpractised in horsemanship, they were now mounted. And since the infantry were few in number and unable even to make a phalanx of any consequence, and had never had the courage to engage with the barbarians, but always turned to flight at the first onset, he considered it unsafe to draw them up at a distance from the fortifications, but thought it best that they should remain in position where they were, close by the moat, his purpose being that, if it should so happen that the Roman horsemen were routed, they should be able to receive the fugitives and, as a fresh body of men, help them to ward off the enemy'.

At first the Romans had the advantage, the Gothic cavalry opposing Belisarius' main force fell back under the pressure of Roman archery. The diversion from the Aurelian gate initially swept all before them. Then as the Roman citizen troops fell into disorder and began to loot the enemy camp the Gothic cavalry turned around and cut them to pieces.

Meanwhile the main Roman force came up against the Gothic infantry who 'protecting themselves with their shields, vigorously warded off their opponents, destroying many men and a much larger number of horses... Finally the horsemen of the barbarians who were on the right wing, taking note of this, advanced at a gallop against the enemy opposite them. And the Romans there, unable to withstand their spears, rushed off in flight and fell back on the infantry phalanx. However, the infantry also were unable to hold their ground against the oncoming horsemen, and most of them began to join the cavalry in flight'.

The siege of Rome dragged on for over a year with constant skirmishes as both sides faced the prospect of starvation and disease. On receiving further reinforcements from Constantinople, Belisarius sent detachments out into the Gothic heartland to the north. When the Romans captured Ariminum (modern Rimini) in their rear, Witiges broke the siege, burned his camps and fell back towards Ravenna.

The Goths wanted to protect their power bases in northern Italy but to do so presented them with a dilemma. Without adequate garrisons the cities would invariably capitulate to the advancing Romans so Witiges was forced to reduce his army by leaving behind several hundred men in each of the important cities he needed to hold. Even the support of 10,000 Burgundians sent by the Frankish king Theudebert was not enough to to swing the balance as Belisarius was also reinforced by 2000 Germanic Heruls and 5000 Roman regulars commanded by Narses. In 540, after a failed diplomatic effort to persuade Belisarius to share power and take on the mantle of West Roman Emperor, Witiges surrendered.

The Lost Peace

The war should have been over. Witiges along with several other Gothic notables and their families were pensioned off after being paraded before Justinian and his courtiers in Constantinople. The Gothic royal treasure was added to the Imperial coffers and Belisarius was sent to the east to deal with a resurgent Persian threat.

The Emperor Justinian apparently learned no lessons from the failure of his policies in Africa after the defeat of the Vandals (recounted in the first book in this series). Having won the war his officials went on to lose the peace. Justinian left eleven separate military commanders scattered in small garrisons throughout Italy with no overall general. Justinian's voracious tax collectors then set about squeezing the country dry. The civilian governor Alexander the Logothete (the auditor) earned the nickname 'snips' due to his propensity to cut coins by trimming the edges. He attempted to collect back taxes theoretically owing from the end of Theodoric's reign while failing to adequately compensate the soldiers who had won the victory.

In modern times we have seen plenty of examples in Iraq, Afghanistan and Libya when relatively swift military victories turned to disaster when not enough attention and resources were spent to create stability and secure peace. So it had been when Justinian's policies in Africa resulted in mutiny and years of continued conflict. The same happened in Italy.

'Hence not only did the Italians become disaffected from the Emperor Justinian, but not one of the soldiers was willing any longer to undergo the dangers of war, and by willfully refusing to fight, they caused the strength of the enemy to grow continually greater'. (Procopius)

North of the Po River there were still a significant number of Goths who had not formally surrendered. As Justinian's officials went about alienating the Italians and the Roman troops they saw an opportunity. Ildibad, commander of the garrison at Verona, was proclaimed king and he went about strengthening his position.

> 'He began to gather about him all the barbarians and as many of the Roman soldiers as were inclined to favour a revolution. And he sought by every means to strengthen his rule, and laboured diligently to recover for the Gothic nation the sovereignty of Italy. Now at the first not more than a thousand men followed him and they held only one city but little by little all the inhabitants of Liguria and Venetia came over to his side'. (Procopius)

Had the Imperial forces in Italy acted swiftly and with a concerted effort they could probably have nipped this in the bud. Instead Vitalius, the commander in Venetia acted alone. His army, consisting mostly of Heruls, was destroyed in battle at Tarbesium (modern Treviso) in 541.

Despite his victory Ildibad did not last long. He was killed by one of his Gepid bodyguards and Eraric, a Rugian, then seized the kingship, proclaiming himself King of the Rugians and assuming command of the free Goths north of the Po. These events show that even at the highest levels of their society not every Ostrogoth was necessarily a Goth by birth as Procopius explains:

> 'Now these Rugians are indeed a Gothic nation, but in ancient times they used to live as an independent people. But Theodoric had early persuaded them, along with certain other nations, to form an alliance with him, and they were absorbed into the Gothic nation and acted in common with them in all things against their enemies. But since they had absolutely no intercourse with women other than their own, each successive generation of children was of unmixed blood, and thus they had preserved the name of their nation among themselves'.

Ildibad's assassination and Eraric's usurpation did not go down well with most of the Goths. Five months later they killed him and proclaimed Ildibad's nephew Totila as their new king. Energetic and skilled in both war and diplomacy, Totila continued what his uncle had begun. He consolidated his position and gathered more men to his standard — Ildibad's initial 1,000 followers growing to 5,000.

It was now clear in Constantinople that the war for Italy was not yet over. Justinian forced his generals to take action. With 12,000 men including Persians, Isaurians, Heruls, Armenians and Moors the Roman army advanced north from Ravenna under its eleven commanders.

The Battle of Faventia, 542 AD

There is not enough space to fully recount the various engagements of the war for Italy. After the paucity of information we have for the many fifth century battles, Procopius' multi volume account of the Gothic War is awash with detail, much of it firsthand. Thanks to the internet much of this is now freely available in translation. Readers interested in learning more would also do well to try to get their hands on Roy Boss' excellent *Justinian's Wars*, now sadly out of print (see bibliography). What I shall do is highlight a number of engagements which best demonstrate different aspects of Gothic warfare. The first battle of Totila's reign is one of these.

In a reversal of the situation when Belisarius first invaded Italy, in 542 it was the Goths who were outnumbered — 12,000 to 5,000. Not that they were all ethnic Goths. Apart from Gepids and Rugians already mentioned, Roman deserters filled their ranks and it is possible that some of the Burgundians sent by the Franks to help Witiges in 538 may have been part of the Gothic force. In 554-5 the Goths were being led by a man of Hun origins if further proof is needed of the multi-ethnic make-up of the Ostrogoths. What the Gothic army had, however, was a united command under a skillful leader who held their respect. They were also fighting for the survival of their independence. The Roman army not only suffered from a disunited command but, as previously mentioned, their soldiers were feeling aggrieved.

After a failed attempt to take Verona the Romans fell back on Faventia (modern Faenza) and Totila advanced against them. Despite the urgings of the firebrand Artabazes, who commanded the Persian troops in the Roman army, the disunited Imperial command did not authorize an active defence of the sort Belisarius conducted during the siege of Rome. Instead they formed up behind the Po River and surrendered the initiative to Totila without attempting to impede the river crossing.

Totila detached 300 men with orders to cross the river 4 kms from his main position and then move around behind the enemy and to attack them from the rear once the main forces were engaged. Then he took the rest of his army across the Po and advanced on the Romans. As the two armies were closing on each other a Gothic champion, 'Valaris by name, tall of stature and of most terrifying mien, an active man and a good fighter, rode his horse out before the rest of the army and took his stand in the open space between the armies, clad in a corselet and wearing a helmet on his head; and he challenged all the Romans, if anyone was willing to do battle with him'.

The challenge was met by Artabazes.

'So they rode their horses toward each other, and when they came close, both thrust their spears, but Artabazes, anticipating his opponent, delivered the first blow and pierced the right side of Valaris. And the barbarian, mortally wounded, was about to fall backward to the earth, but his spear, resting on the ground behind him and being braced against a rock, did not permit him to fall. As for Artabazes, he continued to press forward still more vigorously, driving the spear into the man's vitals; for as yet he did not suppose that he had already suffered a mortal wound. Thus it came about that Valaris' spear stood practically upright and its iron point encountered the corselet of Artabazes, and first, entering little by little, it went clear through the corselet, and then, slipping further, grazed the skin of Artabazes' neck. And by some chance the iron, as it pushed forward, cut an artery which lies in that region, and there was immediately a great flow of blood'. (Procopius)

Such challenges to personal combat were a common feature of sixth century warfare. They appear to have been conducted under an unwritten set of rules. A champion would ride out and issue a challenge which if not accepted would demoralize the enemy. In the case of Roman armies the response was usually made without formal authorization. Inevitably a notable warrior of non-Roman origin would accept and the two armies would stand by to watch how things played out. Winning the duel would boost the morale of the army whose champion had triumphed. In the case of the duel between Valaris and Artabazes, although the latter had won he was mortally wounded and could take no further part in the battle. As Artabazes was perhaps the most talented and aggressive of the eleven Roman commanders on the field, his loss was probably a greater blow to Roman fortunes than the temporary morale boost from his victory.

Totila's men held their own long enough against the enemy numbers to allow the flanking force to arrive in their rear. 'When the Romans saw these men, supposing as they did that their assailants were a great multitude, they fell into a panic and straightway rushed off in flight, each man as best he could. And the barbarians kept up a slaughter of Romans as they fled in complete disorder, and many of them they captured and held under guard, and they captured all the standards besides'.

Totila's victory shows that with good leadership the Ostrogoths were perfectly capable of planning and executing battle-winning tactics which depended on close coordination and timing. Without Belisarius' leadership the fragmented Roman command and the polyglot nature of their army gave them none of the advantages one might expect from a 'civilized' army fighting 'barbarians'. Totila's army was small but all of them would have been experienced soldiers rather than the full levy of the Ostrogoths which Witiges had commanded at the siege of Rome.

Resurgence and Counter Attack

The war dragged on for another decade. For most of this time the Goths were in the ascendancy. They re-took Naples and then moved back north to threaten

Rome. Belisarius was recalled to Italy in 544 but he was given very few troops and was unable to relieve Rome which surrendered to Totila the following year.

Totila's army grew along with his success. We do not know for certain who the men were who swelled his ranks. When Witiges surrendered most of the lower class Goths south of the Po had gone back to their farms more or less undisturbed by the changes at the top. As Totila marched south many of them are likely to have joined him. Many Roman soldiers deserted and several thousand joined Totila.

Totila did not try to hold Rome. He realized that if he did his army would end up being pinned in a place that was difficult to supply. He made some attempts to dismantle the walls to make it harder for the city to be held against him and then moved back towards Ravenna. Rome switched back and forth between Roman and Gothic control as the war continued without any decisive outcome. The fighting on land tended to favour the Goths but their superior navy allowed the Romans to move and land troops with relative ease and at the same time keep their armies re-supplied. This was not enough to defeat the resurgent Goths. Rome once again fell to them, many Roman troops went over to the Gothic side, Belisarius was recalled to Constantinople, and in 550 Totila moved on to recapture Sicily.

Once again it looked as if the war was over. This time the Goths were triumphant having re-established control over most of Italy and Sicily even though the Franks had taken advantage of the war to expand into Venetia. Justinian, however, could not accept the loss of prosperous Sicily as it was a vital bridge to Roman North Africa as well as being an important base to control the sea lanes in the western Mediterranean. Determined to finally bring the war to a satisfactory close he appointed his nephew Germanus to lead a Roman counter-attack and gave him the resources to do it properly — something he had never given Belisarius.

Germanus was a skilful and experienced general who had won victories over Roman mutineers and Vandals in North Africa. He was also a widower and one of the first things he did was to marry Matasuntha, Amalasuntha's daughter. By allying himself to the family of Theodoric the Great he hoped that many of the Goths would be reluctant to take up arms against him. 'The Goths were both frightened and perplexed at the same time, being faced, as they were, with the necessity of making war upon the race of Theodoric'. (Procopius)

With the funds given to him by the Emperor, together with some of his own money, Germanus went about raising an army in Dalmatia with the intent of moving into the Gothic heart lands of northern Italy. Attracted by the cash, household troops of other generals came to join him as did barbarian recruits from along the Danube. Before the expedition could get underway Germanus had to divert to deal with a Slavic incursion across the Danube. He succeeded in defeating the Slavs but shortly afterwards he became ill and died, leaving the army without its capable commander. These delays ensured that the Roman counter-attack could not take place in 550 as it had become too late in the year to risk launching it. So the army went into winter quarters at Salona (near Split in modern Croatia).

This gave Totila and the main Gothic army time to move from Sicily back up to northern Italy to meet the anticipated Roman attack the following spring. '[The Goths] collected as booty a vast number of horses and other animals, and had stripped [Sicily] of grain and all its other crops; these, together with all the treasure, which amounted to a great sum indeed, they loaded on their ships, and then suddenly abandoned the island and returned to Italy'. (Procopius) Leaving behind only small garrisons in four strongholds, Totila reasoned that if he could defeat Germanus' army, command of which eventually fell to the eunuch Narses, then he could later return to Sicily at leisure.

The Goths at Sea

Totila did not wait passively for the Roman counter-attack. He sent a fleet of 300 ships towards Greece with orders to plunder the coastline and to attack any enemy ships. In doing so he hoped to interrupt the Roman seaborne supply routes and challenge their naval superiority in the Adriatic. If he succeeded he would neutralize one of Constantinople's strategic advantages — the ability to move men and supplies quickly by sea from the Dalmatian coast to Italy. The Gothic fleet had some success as Procopius reports. 'Going about the whole coast and meeting many Roman ships, they captured every one of them, cargoes and all. Among these happened to be also some of the ships which were carrying provisions from Greece for the army of Narses'.

No doubt their ships were built and crewed by Romans with Gothic warriors acting as marines. Probably most of them were simple transport ships although dromons — light galleys with a single bank of oars — probably also formed part of the fleet. Although the Goths never took to the sea like the Vandals, Theodoric the Great had begun to realize the necessity of building up a naval capability. Theodoric's letter to Abundantius, his Praetorian Prefect is preserved in Cassidorius' *Variae*.

> 'By Divine inspiration we have determined to raise a navy which may both ensure the arrival of the cargoes of public corn and may, if need be, combat the ships of an enemy. For, that Italy, a country abounding in timber, should not have a navy of her own hath often stricken us with regret. Let your Greatness therefore give directions for the construction of a thousand dromons. Wherever cypresses and pines are found near to the seashore, let them be bought at a suitable price. Then as to the levy of sailors: any fitting man, if a slave, must be hired of his master, or bought

at a reasonable price. If free, he is to receive five solidi as donative, and will have his rations during the term of service. Even those who were slaves are to be treated in the same way, since it is a kind of freedom to serve the Ruler of the State and are to receive, according to their condition, two or three solidi of bounty money. Fishermen, however, are not to be enlisted in this force, since we lose with regret one whose vocation it is to provide us with luxuries; and moreover one kind of training is required for him who has to face the stormy wind, and another for him who need only fish close to shore'.

It is doubtful that such a large fleet was ever constructed and for the greater part of the war for Italy the Goths were not able to really challenge Roman naval superiority and were far less capable fighting at sea than they were on land. This is demonstrated by an engagement which took place when Totila sent a force commanded by Scipuar, Gibal and Gundulf, to re-take Ancon (modern Ancona) probably late in 550 or early 551. Gundulf had previously been one of Belisarius' *bucellarii*, showing the extent to which deserters from the Roman army had been integrated into the Gothic ranks. The army was accompanied by forty-seven ships so as to seal the town by land and sea. The Romans sent a fleet of fifty ships to relieve the siege and a naval battle took place which is described in detail by Procopius.

'The fighting was exceedingly fierce and resembled a battle on land. For both sides set their ships head on with the bows against those of their opponents and discharged their arrows against each other, and all those who laid some claim to valour brought their ships close enough to touch one another and then engaged from the decks, fighting with sword and spear just as if on a plain... The barbarians, through lack of experience in sea-fighting, began to carry on the combat with great disorder; for some of them became so far separated from one another that they gave their enemy opportunity to ram them singly, while others drew together in large groups and were constantly hindered by one another because of the crowding of the boats... They continually collided with each other and then pushed off again with their poles in a disorderly manner, sometimes pushing their prows into the crowded space, and sometimes backing off to a great distance... Consequently the Goths in great disorder turned to a disgraceful retreat'.

Only eleven ships survived. Under Gundulf's command the Goths landed and then set fire to their ships to prevent their capture. On foot the crews linked up with the land forces around Ancon and together they abandoned the siege and retreated to Auximus (modern Osimo).

Procopius says that Gothic morale was shaken by the defeat at Ancon and that Totila sent envoys to Justinian asking for peace. He offered to cede Dalmatia and Sicily to the Empire and expressed willingness to pay taxes and serve in the Roman army in return for being allowed to remain in control of Italy. Justinian rebuffed Totila's overtures and so the stage was set for the final show-down.

The Battle of Taginae, 552 AD

Narses had taken command of Germanus' army and with additional funding he augmented it. He brought with him a strong force of regular Roman soldiers from Constantinople, Thrace and Illyricum. The Lombard ruler Auduin provided 2,500 well equipped warriors supported by 3,000 lesser men to join Narses. 3,000 Herul cavalry, 400 Gepids as well as Huns and Persian deserters swelled the ranks of the Roman army. Probably numbering in the region of 25,000 to 30,000 men it was by far the largest army marshalled by Justinian in his attempts to restore Imperial authority over the West. It certainly outnumbered the troops Totila could marshal to oppose it. Even with the Roman deserters who augmented his forces it is unlikely that Totila could muster more than 20,000 men, probably less.

Both sides made overtures to the Franks in Venetia. Totila was able to secure their neutrality if not their active support. Justinian failed to get the Franks to join him or even to allow his army to pass unhindered into Italy. Narses, however, was able to move around the Frankish strongholds to reach Ravenna in the spring of 552. He then bypassed the Gothic garrisoned towns to advance on Rome. Totila marched out to meet him and took up a position at Taginae (modern Gualdo Tadino). He was awaiting reinforcements of 2,000 cavalry so Totila sought to delay and seize the tactical advantage. He sent a mounted force to take a hill from which he hoped to outflank the Romans. Narses had previously sent a detachment of fifty men to occupy it and against the odds they held out against the Gothic horsemen.

Procopius' account of this engagement is interesting as it shows how a small force of determined men on foot with spears and bows could hold off repeated charges by mounted men. It also shows that the Ostrogothic horsemen were less inclined than their forefathers to dismount to fight on foot even when the tactical circumstances favoured dismounted combat.

'The Romans drew up together into a small space and, making a barrier with their shields and thrusting forward their spears, held their ground. Then the Goths came on, charging in haste and thus getting themselves into disorder, while the fifty, pushing with their shields and thrusting very rapidly with their spears... defended themselves most vigorously against their assailants; and they purposely made a din with their shields, terrifying the horses, on the one hand by this means, and the men, on the other, with the points of their spears. And the horses became excited, because they were greatly troubled both by the rough ground and by the din of the shields, and also because they could not get through anywhere, while the men at the same time were gradually worn out, fighting as they were with men packed so closely together and not giving an inch of ground, and trying to manage horses that did not in the least obey their urging… [The Romans] stretched their bows and kept shooting with a most telling aim at the enemy. And they destroyed many men and many horses as well, as long as their quivers still held arrows'.

Having failed to take the hill Totila deployed his army for battle while still delaying to await the expected reinforcements. With the two armies lined up against each other Coccas, one of the Roman deserters in the Gothic army, rode out and issued a challenge to single combat. This was met by the Armenian Anzalas from the Roman army who defeated him.

The Romans were encouraged by this but neither side advanced on the other. Still seeking to delay battle while awaiting his reinforcements Totila rode out into the space between the two armies.

'He [Totila] was not at all reluctant to make an exhibition to the enemy of what manner of man he was. For the armour in which he was clad was abundantly plated with gold and the ample adornments which hung from his cheek-plates as well as from his helmet and spear were not only of purple but in other respects befitting a king, marvelous in their abundance. And he himself, sitting upon a very large horse, began to perform the dance under arms skilfully between the armies. For he wheeled his horse round in a circle and then turned him again to the other side and so made him run round and round. And as he rode he hurled his javelin into the air and caught it again as it quivered above him, then passed it rapidly from hand to hand, shifting it with consummate skill, and he gloried in his practice in such matters'.

The Gothic reinforcements arrived as both sides were relaxing in their ranks and eating their midday rations. Totila re-armed himself in the dress of an ordinary soldier and hoping to catch the Romans unawares he immediately led the Goths forward into the attack. All his cavalry were deployed in the front ranks with the infantry behind to provide a secure base which the Gothic cavalry could fall back on and re-group if the initial charges proved unsuccessful.

Narses was not caught unawares. He had his men eat a small meal in their ranks with their equipment on and with orders to expect an attack at any time. He had deployed in a crescent with his infantry augmented by dismounted Lombards and Heruls in the centre. 8,000 'unmounted archers' were split between the two flanks, supported by mounted cavalry. Narses took his position on the Roman left wing with his own *bucellarii*, the better regular Roman cavalry and the Huns. 1,500 of these men were held back as a reserve. 500 of them had orders to intervene to block any enemy breakthrough while the remaining 1,000 were to wait until the infantry were engaged and then outflank the enemy infantry.

The Roman archers on the wings may either have been in front of the cavalry or on the extreme flanks. When the Gothic cavalry attacked they were enfiladed by archery from the wings so this may indicate that the archers were deployed on the far ends of the battle line. Unsupported units of archers could have been easily ridden down by the Gothic horsemen. This has led to some historians, notably Oman, to conclude that they were deployed in front of the cavalry so the latter could charge through their ranks to meet an attack.

There is, however, a strong possibility that the archers on the Roman flanks were not light foot archers but rather dismounted bow-armed cavalry. In this case they would have worn armour and been equipped for close combat with spears and good swords in addition to their bows. If this was the case then the front rank could have been spear-armed, perhaps with larger shields while the rear ranks shot with their bows. 'The Roman wings, in each of which 4,000 unmounted horsemen had taken their stand, were moved forward at Narses' command so as to form a crescent'. (Procopius) These 4,000 dismounted cavalry on each wing could only have been the same as the 8,000 'unmounted archers' mentioned earlier.

Totila launched a full frontal assault aiming to break the centre of the enemy line with a ferocious cavalry charge. In previous engagements, such as Faventia previously described, Tolitla had shown that he was perfectly capable of tactical finesse. Yet at Taginae he showed none. Even Procopius is at a loss to describe why this was.

> 'Now orders had been given to the entire Gothic army that they should use neither bow not any other weapon in battle except their spears. Consequently it came about that Totila was out-generalled by his own folly; for in entering this battle he was led, by what I do not know, to throw against his opponents his one army with inadequate equipment and outflanked'.

Perhaps, knowing that he was outnumbered, outflanked and facing an opponent using combined arms, he realized that he could not hope to win a drawn out engagement. Therefore he relied on the one thing his men did better than the Romans and that was to deliver a ferocious charge. Over the past decade his men had more success than failure in the field and he was no doubt hoping that this would carry him through again. The fact that Totila had taken the time to change from his gilded, plumed armour to don the equipment of an ordinary warrior is possibly an indication that he thought his chances were slim.

The battle was a disaster for the Goths. Raked by archery from the flanks they had no chance of breaking through the steady ranks of dismounted Lombards and Heruls. They fell back, quite possibly re-grouped and then tried again. Eventually the Gothic cavalry retreated, not in an orderly retirement but in full rout. The infantry failed to hold their ground and were also swept up in the rout. The Romans gave no quarter. Totila was killed alongside 6,000 of his men.

The End of the Ostrogoths

The Battle of Taginae broke the power of the Ostrogoths. The survivors, led by Teisas, marched south towards Cumae where the Gothic royal treasure was being held by Teisas' brother Aligern. Cumae was being besieged by a Roman force but Teisas was unable to break the siege as Narses was hard on his heels. After two months of indecisive skirmishing and failed attempts to get the Franks to intervene on their behalf, the Goths fell back on Mons Lactarius (modern Monti Lattari near Naples). In 533 they made one last heroic stand, dismounting and launching an assault on foot against superior Roman numbers, in the manner of their ancestors.

'Teisas, easily recognized by all, stood with only a few followers at the head of the phalanx, holding his shield before him and thrusting forward his spear. And when the Romans saw this… they all directed their spears at him, some thrusting while others hurled them. He himself, meanwhile, covered by his shield, received all their spears in it, and by sudden charges he slew a large number. And whenever he saw his shield was filled with spears fixed in it, he would hand it over to one of his guards and take another for himself… As if fastened to the ground he stood there, shield in hand, killing with his right hand and parrying with his left. [When he turned to take a new shield from one of his bodyguards] his chest became exposed for a brief instant of time and it chanced that at that moment he was hit by a javelin and died instantly'. (Procopius)

This was a fitting end to the last king of the Ostrogoths — dying in doomed, heroic combat. The war in Italy continued as the Franks finally moved in, not to help the Goths but to take if for themselves. They too were defeated by Narses in

554 but a force of 7,000 Goths still remained free under the leadership of a Hun by the name of Ragnaris. These were subdued in 555 when Ragnaris was killed after a failed negotiation with Narses. The last remnants of Gothic resistance were wiped out in 561-2 when a revolt led by Widin, supported by the Franks, was crushed by Narses.

It took Justinian twenty-eight years to re-conquer Italy and destroy the vibrant Romano-Gothic kingdom which Theodoric the Great had created. It was a hollow victory. Whatever blending of Germanic and Roman cultures had begun at the end of the fifth century had been wiped out by the middle of the sixth. The last vestiges of ancient Roman life had been utterly destroyed by three decades of constant warfare. In 568 the Lombards moved into the vacuum and took Italy for themselves.

Chapter 11

The Gothic Epilogue

Visigoths and Romans

In Chapter 8 we left the Visigoths in Spain at the death of their Ostrogothic king Theudis in 548. This was at the height of the Ostrogothic resurgence in Italy under Totila's leadership.

Following a depressingly familiar pattern the Visigoths were no more united than their Ostrogothic cousins before Totila. Theudis was assassinated and succeeded by Theudisgisel who only lasted a year before being assassinated in turn by Agila. In 551 the citizens of Cordoba rose up in revolt and managed to hold their own against attempts by Agila to subdue them. Taking advantage of the situation, Athanagild made a bid for power and called for support from Constantinople.

Why Justinian decided to divert resources from the bitter conflict in Italy at the same time he was fighting a war against Persia on the eastern frontiers is hard to fathom, but he did. In 552 he sent a naval force initially earmarked to retake Sicily from the Ostrogoths on to Spain. Probably Justinian hoped to take the Spanish ports to protect his North African conquests while hoping that Narses' army would be enough to secure Italy and Sicily. Unlike the invasions of Africa and Italy the Roman intervention in Spain was an attempt to secure important bases on the southeast coast rather than to re-conquer the province.

It turned out that Justinian's judgement was correct. As Narses was defeating Totila the Roman fleet landed troops and captured Malaga. Then in alliance with Athanagild they took Baza, Segontia and Cartagena. With Roman support Athanagild was able to defeat Agila and become King of the Visigoths even though he was unable to suppress the Cordoban revolt. The Cordobans managed to take Seville and maintained their independence until 572 when they were finally brought back under control by King Leovigild.

By the time of his death in 586, Leovigild had defeated various self-governing enclaves; saw off an attack by the Franks; suppressed bands of *bacaudae*; contained the Imperial Roman garrisons; and brought most of the Spanish peninsula under royal control, including the remnants of the Suevic Kingdom. The Roman garrisons hung on to the coast until 625 when Cartagena, the administrative centre of the Imperial province of Spain, finally fell to the Visigoths under Suinthila.

A full melding of Gothic and Roman societies, both in Italy and Spain, was hampered by religious differences. The Goths were Arians and their Roman subjects were Nicene Catholics. While both the Ostrogoths and Visigoths were far more tolerant of these religious differences than the Vandals, they still served to keep both communities apart.

As the Visigothic kings re-established their authority they realized that this was a problem than needed solving. There were probably very few Arians in late sixth century Spain other than the Visigothic aristocrats and the clergy. Their adherence to the Arian form of Christianity was probably less due to deeply held religious beliefs than a sense of shared identity from which power flowed. Some of the Visigoths converted over the years and the Arian clergy adapted their theology to come closer to the Catholic belief that God the father and son were equal.

In 587 King Reccared, who had succeeded his father Leovigild the year before, converted to Catholicism. Two years later Reccared and his queen Baddo assembled seventy-two bishops, the Visigothic nobility and others at the Third Council of Toledo. The result was the end of the Arian version of Christianity. From this point onward the Visigoths and Romans shared the same religion and the seeds were sown from which a new Spanish identity eventually evolved.

For the next 120 years Visigothic Spain was relatively stable. There was plenty of conflict as the various nobles competed for power and the Franks beyond the Pyrenees were a constant menace. No hereditary royal family emerged and the Visigothic nobles continued to elect their king from amongst their number. Real power, therefore, lay with the important noble families whose estates were spread throughout the kingdom and not with the court at Toledo.

The Arab Conquest

In the early 630s the Arabs, united under a new religion inspired by the Prophet Mohammed, began to expand out of the Arabian Peninsula. Their first targets were the East Roman and Persian Empires. They defeated the East Roman Emperor Heraclius at the Battle of Yarmuk in 635 and took Syria. Alexandria fell in 642 and by 698 they had taken Carthage, ending Roman control of North Africa. From there the Arabs took control of the Western Mediterranean raiding Sicily, Sardinia and the Balearic Isles. Ceuta, on the promontory across the straights from Spain, fell to the Arabs in 706.

If there was ever a time the Visigothic nobles needed to stand together this was it. Instead Ruderic overthrew King Wittiza and seized the throne in a violent coup. What happened next is confusing but it is clear that Ruderic did not have unanimous support of the nobles. Another noble, Achila, was minting coins proclaiming him as king at the same time as Ruderic. Wittiza' sons also contested the kingship.

It seems likely that the Arabs who crossed over from Africa to Spain in 711 were invited or encouraged by those who opposed Ruderic's rule. It was an eerie parallel to the political machinations of the later Roman Empire where one faction would call in a group of barbarians to support their bid for power and were left with a strong army in their midst which could no longer be controlled. So it was that the Visigoths fell to the same sort of forces which had brought their ancestors to power.

The number of Arabs and Berbers who moved into Spain was relatively small, probably less than 10,000 men. Ruderic could have called on many more but he did not have the full support of his kingdom and the Visigoths were no longer set up to conduct total war. Since Leogivild's re-assertion of control at the end of the sixth century the Visigoths did not have to deal with any serious threats. Their armies were geared to deal with banditry, local revolts and skirmishes with the Franks on the northern frontier. For generations they had no experience of dealing with a determined enemy.

Led by Tariq bin Ziyad, an army of Arabs and Berbers defeated and killed Ruderic in 711 and then went on to capture Toledo. In a very brief campaign the Visigothic Kingdom of Spain was overthrown and the Goths passed from history.

The Gothic Legacy

Of all the Germanic peoples, the Goths had by far the greatest impact on the later Roman Empire. The Gothic migration of 376 was not the first major barbarian incursion into Roman territory, nor was it the last. Despite the tendency of modern historians to downplay such things I do believe that the Battle of Adrianople in 378 was indeed a turning point in history. Not only did the Goths defeat the Roman army and kill the Emperor on home territory, they managed to hold out to achieve a settlement without ever being defeated in battle. This settlement may not have been all that every warrior who fought at Adrianople might have hoped for but it succeeded in breaking the mould.

Prior to Adrianople initial barbarian successes inevitably ended in defeat and punitive expeditions against their home territory. Fritigen's Goths had abandoned their home territory, were not defeated and they soon learned that a few thousand of their determined warriors could not only overrun the hard pressed frontier regions but that they could swing the balance in a Roman civil war.

This lesson was learned not only by their descendants but also by other barbarian tribes over the frontier, including other Goths who had not joined this initial migration. Despite its huge resources and the many men it had under arms, the Roman Empire became increasingly dependent on relatively small numbers of semi-independent Goths and other barbarians to man their armies. Some, such as Gainas, sought a traditional route to power by rising up through the ranks of the Roman establishment. Others, like Alaric and Theodoric the Great, found that they could take what they needed when the Romans did not give them what they demanded.

The Goths did not cause the end of the Roman Empire in the West but they were certainly a contributing factor. Alaric's descendants took southwestern France for themselves and then expanded into Spain, while Theodoric took Italy. There was Roman collusion in both instances so they were not conquests in the traditional sense. The Gothic armies were seen by many as nothing more than barbarians in the service of Rome and the more enlightened Gothic leaders were careful to keep the powerful Roman aristocrats on their side. Under Theodoric in Italy there was a brief flowering of a Romano–Gothic Empire under which Roman laws and traditions continued while Gothic soldiers maintained the peace and expanded control over Dalmatia, Provence and Spain.

So, despite the title of this series of books, the Goths were not really 'conquerors of Rome'. If anything, their best rulers sought to preserve Rome rather than destroy her. It did not last, thanks to several factors. The first was the expansion of the Franks which broke the back of the Visigoths, the second was disunity amongst the Goths themselves following the death of Alaric II of the Visigoths and Theodoric the Great of the Ostrogoths. The final straw was the three decades long war in which Justinian managed briefly to re-establish Roman control over Africa, Italy and parts of Spain. In doing so he actually managed to destroy the last vestiges of the West Roman Empire which the Goths had partially preserved.

Chronology

166-180: The Marcomanic Wars.

235-284: Upheaval and endemic civil war in the Roman Empire.

238-250: Gothic raids across the Danube.

251: Cniva's Goths destroy the Roman army at Arbutus, killing the Emperor Decius.

253: Renewed Gothic raids across the Danube.

254: First seaborne raids across the Black Sea by the Borani and Goths.

255: Plague in the Roman Empire. Persians invade the East.

260: Sassanid Persians defeat and capture the Emperor Valerian.

267-8: Goths and Heruls launch new amphibious attacks. Athens sacked.

269: Claudius II defeats the Goths at the Battle of Naissus.

270: Aurelian defeats Cannabaudes and leads punitive expedition against the Goths.

276 Probus defeats Gothic raiders.

284-305: Reign of Diocletian. Order restored in the Roman Empire.

306-337: Reign of Constantine the Great.

332: Constantine defeats the Tervingi, takes hostages and concludes a peace treaty with them.

341: Ulfilas begins to convert the Goths to Arian Christianity.

349: Goths serve in the Roman army against the Persians.

363: Julian's invasion of Persia ends in disaster and the death of the Emperor.

365 Goths support the usurper Procopius against Valens.

367-69: Valens conducts punitive expeditions against the Goths.

c.370-374: The Huns defeat the Alans, pushing them westward.

373-375: Renewed war between Rome and Persia.

375-6: Huns move into Gothic territory sending refugees south and westward.

376: Gothic refugees seek asylum inside Roman territory.

376: Bungled assassination attempt on Fritigern and Alatheus triggers Gothic revolt.

376: Goths defeat Lupicinus at the Battle of Marcianople. They equip themselves from Roman armouries.

377: Romans fail to defeat Goths, Huns and Alans at the Battle of Ad Salices.

378, 9 August: The Goths destroy the East Roman army at the Battle of Adrianople.

382, October: Goths settled in the Balkans under treaty with Theodosius.

382: Magnus Maximus proclaimed emperor in Britain. Moving to Gaul, he establishes his capital at Trier.

386: A Gruethungi incursion is defeated by the Romans. The survivors are resettled as military colonists in Asia Minor.

388: Magnus Maximus defeated by Theodosius who calls on the Goths to help him.

392: Death of Valentinian II. Arbogast proclaims Eugenius emperor.

394: Eugenius and Arbogast defeated by Theodosius, supported by a large number of Goths, at the Battle of Frigidus River.

395: Death of Theodosius. The Roman Empire divided with the West under Honorius and the East under Arcadius. Stilicho holds supreme power. Alaric leads a rebellion of Goths in the Balkans.

396: Alaric's Goths plunder Greece and Thrace.

397: Constantinople refuses Stilicho's aid against Alaric. Alaric is appointed *Magister Militum per Illyricum* by the East Roman Emperor.

399: Tribigild's Greuthungi rebel in Asia Minor.

c.400: Huns move further west, settling on the Hungarian plain and triggering off another wave of Germanic migrations.

400: Gainas defeated by Fravitta. Goths massacred in Constantinople.

401: Alaric invades Italy for the first time but is driven back.

405: Radagasius invades Italy, his army including large numbers of Goths.

406, 23 August: Radagasius defeated by Stilicho near Florence.

406: British army revolts proclaiming Constantine III as emperor.

406, 31 December: Vandals, Suevi and Alans cross the Rhine.

407: Constantine III crosses into Gaul. Constantine's forces keep the Vandals and their allies bottled up in northern Gaul.

407-8: Vandals, Alans, Suevi, Burgundians and Alamanni overrun much of Gaul.

408, 22 August: Stilicho executed. Alaric again invades Italy. Soldiers from Stilicho's army desert and join Alaric.

408-409: Alaric blockades Rome and proclaims Priscus Attalus as emperor.

409: The Vandals, Alans and Suevi cross into Spain.

410, 20 August: Alaric's Goths sack Rome.

411 or late 410: Alaric dies and is succeeded by Athaulf.

411: Honorius's general Constantius defeats Constantine III in Gaul.

412: Athaulf's Goths move into southern Gaul.

414: The Goths move against the Vandals, Alans and Suevi in Spain. They capture Barcelona.

414: Athaulf marries Galla Placidia and proclaims Priscus Attalus as emperor.

415: Athaulf murdered and succeeded by Wallia who returns Galla Placidia to Ravenna and concludes a peace treaty. The Goths move against the barbarians in Spain on behalf of the Romans.

415- 418: Successful campaign by the Goths in Spain resulting in the destruction of the Siling Vandals and the decimation of the Alans.

418: The Goths are settled in Aquitaine. Wallia is murdered and Theodoric I becomes king.

422: Renewed Visigoth campaign against the Vandals on behalf of the Romans.

423: Honorius dies.

425: The 6-year-old Valentinian III becomes Western Emperor with his mother Galla Placidia the power behind the throne.

425: Visigothic attack on Arles fails.

427: Power struggle between Boniface, Felix and Aetius for control of the Western Empire.

429: The Vandals cross over to Africa.

430: Another failed Visigothic attempt to take Arles.

433: Rua, King of the Huns dies and is succeeded by Attila and Bleda. Aetius is given supreme military power in the West.

435: Rebellion of the *bacaudae* in northwestern Gaul.

436: Defeat of the Burgundians by Aetius' Hun allies.

436-9: Conflict between the Visigoths and Romans in Gaul.

439: The Vandals capture Carthage.

441-2: Huns raid throughout the Balkans.

445: Bleda murdered. Attila becomes sole King of the Huns.

447: Attila's Huns again ravage the Balkans and threaten Constantinople.

451: Attila defeated by Visigoths and Romans at the Battle of the Catalaunian Fields near Troyes in France.

452: Attila invades Italy.

453: Death of Attila.

454: The Huns are defeated at the the Battle of Nedao by a coalition of Germanic tribes. Aetius is murdered by Valentinian III.

454-70: The Ostrogoths settled in Pannonia, expand their territory at the expense of their Germanic neighbours.

455: Valentinian murdered.

455: The Vandals sack Rome.

455: Avitus proclaimed Western Emperor with the support of the Goths.

457: Avitus abdicates and is replaced by Majorian with Ricimer the power behind the throne.

457: Supported by Goths settled in Thrace and led by Theodoric Strabo, Aspar places Leo on the East Roman throne.

461: Majorian executed by Ricimer after the failure of a naval expedition against the Vandals.

462: Narbonne ceded to the Visigoths prompting a revolt by the Roman army in Gaul led by Aegidius. The Goths defeat Aegidius and expand north into the Loire valley.

468: The Battle of Mercurium. The Vandals destroy a huge Roman invasion fleet off the coast of Africa.

470: The Ostrogothic king Valamir killed in battle against the Suevi and Scirri.

471: The Thracian Goths rise in revolt when Aspar is assassinated.

471: Theodoric, son of Thiudimir is sent home after a decade as a hostage in Constantinople.

473: Ostrogoths under Thiudimir and Theodoric cross the Balkans to invade Thrace and Greece. Other follow Vidimir to join up with the Visigoths in Gaul.

473: Constantinople concludes a peace with Theodoric Strabo's Thracian Goths

474: Theodoric becomes King of the Ostrogoths on the death of his father Thiudimir.

475: Orestes, Attila's former secretary, proclaims his son Romulus Augustulus West Roman Emperor.

476: Odoacer leads a mutiny of the barbarian troops in the Roman army of Italy. He overthrows Romulus and becomes King of Italy.

476: The Eastern Emperor Zeno transfers the title of Magister Militum from Theodoric Strabo to Theodoric, Thiudimir's son.

476-478: Conflict between the two Theodorics.

481: Death of Theodoric Strabo.

488: Theodoric's Ostrogoths defeat the Gepids on the Ulca River.

489: Ostrogoths under Theodoric invade Italy.

493, March: Theodoric overthrows Odoacer and becomes King of Italy.

494: Visigoths start expanding into Spain.

502-5: War between Persia and the Eastern Empire.

507: The Visigoths in Gaul defeated by the Franks at the Battle of Vouillé. King Alaric II killed. Ostrogothic intervention props up the Visigoths. Amalaric becomes King of the Visigoths with Theodoric the Ostrogoth acting a regent.

519: Euphoric, Theodoric the Great's son-in-law, shares the consulship with the East Roman Emperor Justin.

526, 30 August: Death of Theodoric the Great, King of the Ostrogoths. He is succeeded by his 8-year-old grandson Athalaric with his mother Amalasuntha as regent.

527-565: Reign of Justinian in the Eastern Empire.

531: King Almalaric defeated and killed by the Franks at Barcelona. The Ostrogoth Theudis becomes the next Visigothic king.

533: Belisarius' East Romans invade Africa and capture Carthage.

534: On the death of her son, Amalasuntha supports her cousin Theodahad to become King of the Ostrogoths.

535: Belisarius invades Sicily.

535: The East Roman general Mundo defeats the Ostrogoths in Dalmatia but is later driven out by a Gothic counter-attack.

536: Belisarius invades Italy, takes Naples and Rome. The Ostrogothic nobles depose Theodahad and proclaim Witiges as king.

537: Witiges besieges Rome.

538: Witiges lifts the siege of Rome and falls back on Ravenna. The Romans capture Ariminum.

539: Burgundians, sent by the Franks to aid the Ostrogoths, move into northern Italy. Belisarius is reinforced by Narses.

540: Witiges surrenders. Ildibad becomes King of the Ostrogoths.

541: Ildibad defeats Vitalius at Tarbesium. He is assassinated by his Gepid bodyguard. The Rugian Eraric takes his place. Eraric is assassinated five months later. Totila is proclaimed King of the Ostrogoths.

542: Totila defeats the Romans at Faventia.

543: Goths re-take Naples.

544: Belisarius returns to Italy but can make no headway against the resurgent Ostrogoths.

546: The Goths re-take Rome.

548: Theudis, King of the Visigoths assassinated. Succeeded by Theudisgisel.

549: Theudisgisel assassinated and replaced by Agila.

550: Totila invades Sicily.

550: Germanus appointed to command Roman counter-attack in Italy. He is delayed by a Slavic incursion and dies of disease shortly after.

551: Narses appointed to replace Germanus.

551: Totila's fleet raids Greece and captures Roman re-supply ships. Gothic fleet defeated off Ancona.

551: Cordoba revolts against the authority of the Visigothic king Agila. Athanagild makes a bid for power and calls on Constantinople for support.

552: Narses invades Italy from the North. He defeats Totila at the Battle of Taginae. Teisas becomes King of the Ostrogoths.

552: East Roman troops land in Spain in support of Athanagild. With their support Athanagild overthrows Agila to become King of the Visigoths. The Romans hold on to a coastal strip with Cartagena as their administrative capital.

553: Teisas defeated at Mons Lactarius.

554: Franks invade Italy and are defeated by Narses at Casilinum.

555: The remaining free Ostrogoths defeated by Narses after the death of their leader, the Hun Ragnaris.

561-2: Failed Ostrogothic revolt against Roman rule led by Widin.

568: Lombard invasion of Italy.

572: The Visigothic king Leovigild brings Cordoba back under royal control.

587: The Visigothic king Reccared converts to Catholicism.

589: The Third Council of Toledo convened which ends Arian Christianity in Spain.

625: The East Romans driven out of Spain by the Visigoths.

635: Arabs defeat the East Roman Emperor Heraclius at Yarmuk.

640: The Arabs conquer Egypt.

647: The Arabs invade Roman North Africa.

698: The Arabs capture and destroy Carthage.

706: The Arabs take Ceuta.

711: An Arab and Berber army led by Tariq bin Ziyad, defeats and kills the Visigoth king Ruderic and goes on to capture Toledo.

The Visgothic Kings

Alaric I (395–410)
Athaulf (411–415)
Sigeric (415)
Wallia (415–419)
Theodoric I (419–451)
Thorismund (451–453)
Theodoric II (453–466)
Euric (466–484)
Alaric II (484–507)
Gesalec (507–511)
Amalaric (511–531), Theodoric the Great as regent
Theudis (531–548)
Theudigisel (548–549)
Agila I (549–554)
Athanagild (554–568)
Liuva I (568–569)
Liuvigild (569–586)
Reccared I (586–601)
Liuva II (601–603)
Witteric (603–610)
Gundemar (610–612)
Sisebut (612–621)
Reccared II (621)
Suinthila (621–631)
Reccimer (626–631)
Sisenand (631–636)
Chintila (636–640)
Tulga (640–641)
Chindasuinth (641–653)

Recceswinth or Reccesuinth (649–672)
Wamba (672–680)
Erwig (680–687)
Egica (687–702)
Wittiza (694–710)
Ruderic or Roderic (710–711)

The Ostrogothic Kings

Valamir (unkown–c470)
Thiudimir (c470–474)
Theodoric the Great (474–526)
Athalaric (526–534) Amalasuntha as regent
Theodahad (534–536)
Witiges (536–540)
Ildibad (540–541)
Eraric the Rugian (541)
Totila (541–552)
Teisas (552–553)
Ragnaris the Hun (c554–555)

The Later Roman Emperors

Philip the Arab (244-49)

Decius (249-5) Killed by the Goths at the Battle of Abritus.

Gallus (251-3) Decius's general who may have colluded with the Goths.

Valerian (253-60) Captured by the Persians at the Battle of Edessa.

Gallienus (253-68) Initially co-ruler with Valerian. He campaigned against the Goths in the latter part of his reign. Is credited with reforming the Roman cavalry to make it more effective.

Claudius Gothicus (268-70) Defeated the Goths at the Battle of Naissus then died of plague.

Aurelian (270-5) Continued the war against the Goths and after defeating them led a punitive expedition over the Danube.

Tacitus (275-6) Continued to campaign against the Goths.

Probus (276-82)

Carus (282-3)

Carinus (283-5) Western Emperor.

Numerian (283-4) Eastern Emperor, died on campaign against the Persians.

Diocletian (284-305) Restored order to the Roman Empire and reorganised the government.

Constantine the Great (306-337) Made Christianity the official religion. Campaigned against the Goths over the Danube.

Constantine II (337-40)

Constans (337-50)

Constantius II (337-61)

Julian (261-4) Died on campaign against the Persians.

Jovian (363-4)

Valentinian I (364-75) West Roman Emperor.

Valens (364-78) East Roman Emperor who lost his life at the Battle of Adrianople.

Gratian (375-83) West Roman Emperor who sent troops to aid Valens against the Goths.

Theodosius I (379-395) The last emperor to rule the whole empire.

Magnus Maximus (383-8). British usurper, defeated by Theodosius with the aid of the Goths.

Valentinian II (383-92) West Roman Emperor.

Eugenius (392-4) Western usurper put on the throne by Arbogast and defeated by Theodosius and the Goths at the Battle of Frigidus.

Arcadius (383-408). Initially co-emperor with his father Theodosius and then sole emperor of the East from 395.

Honorius (393-423). Initially co-emperor with his father Theodosius and then sole emperor of the West from 395.

Constantine III (407-411). Proclaimed emperor by the British army he moved into Gaul to establish control over Britain, Gaul and Spain, leaving Honorius controlling only Italy and Africa. Briefly recognised to counter Alaric he was defeated by Honorius' general Constantius in 411.

Priscus Attalus (409 and also 414-415) A usurper who was twice proclaimed emperor by the Visigoths and deposed by Honorius' armies.

Jovinus (411-413) A usurper who briefly filled the vacuum after Constantine III's overthrow in Gaul. He was initially supported by Athaulf's Goths.

Theodosius II (408-450) Eastern Emperor and son of Arcadius.

Constantius III (421). Honorius' general and son-in-law of Theodosius I who was briefly recognised as co-emperor by Honorius.

Joannes (423-425) Proclaimed Emperor of the West after Honorius' death and supported by Aetius, he was deposed by Theodosius II's army.

Valentinian III (425-455) Son of Constantius III and Galla Placidia who was Honorius' sister. He became West Roman Emperor when he was only six years old. Galla Placidia ruled as the power behind the throne before he came of age.

Marcian (450-457). East Roman Emperor. After the end of the Hun Empire he recognized the Ostrogothic settlement in Pannonia.

Petronius Maximus (455). Assumed the Western throne on Valentinian III's death and was killed by the Roman mob when the Vandals sailed to sack Rome.

Avitus (455-456). A Gallo-Roman aristocrat proclaimed Western Emperor with the backing of the Visigoths and deposed by Ricimer.

Majorian (457-461). Made Western Emperor by Ricimer and then deposed after the failure of his attempt to re-conquer Africa from the Vandals.

Leo I (457-474). A soldier who was made East Roman Emperor by Aspar, supported by the Ostrogoths.

Libius Severus (461-465). Made Western Emperor by Ricimer but not recognized by the East.

Anthemius (467-472). An Eastern senator who became Emperor as a result of a deal between Ricimer and Leo. He was deposed by Ricimer.

Olybrius (472) Western Emperor.

Glycerius (473-474) Proclaimed Western Emperor by the Burgundian Gundobad and deposed by the armies of the Eastern Empire.

Julius Nepos (474-475) Put on the Western throne by the Eastern Emperor Leo.

Leo II (474). Eastern Emperor.

Zeno (474-491). Leo I's son-in-law. He was deposed by Basilicus in 475 but regained the throne in 476. He played off the two Ostrogothic factions against each other, eventually sending Theodoric into Italy against Odoacer.

Basilicus (475-476). A general and brother-in-law of Leo I who briefly seized the Eastern throne from Zeno.

Romulus Augustulus (475-467). The last West Roman Emperor, placed on the throne by his father Orestes who had been Attila the Hun's secretary. He was deposed by the Italian army under Odoacer.

Anastasius I (491-518). Another of Leo I's sons-in-law.

Justin (518-527). Commander of Anastasius' bodyguard who was proclaimed emperor by the army.

Justinian (527-565). Justin's nephew who re-conquered Africa from the Vandals and Italy from the Ostrogoths.

Glossary

Alamanni (also Alemanni): A Germanic tribe living on the upper Rhine.

Alans: A nomadic Sarmatian people who originated to the north of the Black Sea. Some of them fought with the Goths at Adrianople. Others later merged with the Vandals.

Arian: Followers of a version of Christianity initially proposed by Arius, which was preached to the Goths and other Germans by Ulfilas in the fourth century. It held that Jesus was from God but not the same as God the Father. It was declared heretical at the council of Nicaea in 325.

Auxilia: Auxiliary units of the later Roman army.

Auxilia Palatina: Elite auxiliaries capable of fighting skirmish actions as well as in the main line of battle.

Baccaudae: A name given to native Romans who had broken from Imperial control to run their own affairs. There were endemic Baccaudae uprisings throughout the fifth century in Gaul and Spain.

Barritus: A war cry used by the Romans, quite possibly adopted from Germanic tribesmen.

Borani: A tribe mentioned by Jordanes as conducting the first seaborne raids across the Black Sea in the third century. They may have been Goths.

Bucellarii: Soldiers forming the personal bodyguards and private armies of late Roman generals. The name comes from *bucellatum* which was a hard tack biscuit forming part of a soldier's rations. Such troops were maintained by the commander himself rather than by the state.

Burgundians: A Germanic people living on the middle Rhine in the early fifth century.

Carpi: The original inhabitants of modern Moldavia, probably related to the Dacians. They were displaced and absorbed by the Goths in the third–fourth centuries.

Catafractarii: Very heavily armoured Roman cavalry units probably modelled on the Sarmatians. They were armed with lances and often rode armoured horses.

Cernjachov culture: The name given by archeologists to the artefacts found in the area north of the Black Sea where the Goths settled in the second-third century AD.

Comes (**Count**): A senior Roman officer who commanded troops of the regional field armies.

Comitatenses: Units of the Roman regional field armies.

Contus: A long two handed lance used on horseback without a shield. Used by the Sarmatians and possibly some Ostrogoths.

Contarii: Roman cavalry units armed with the *contus*.

Dacia: A Roman province roughly equating to modern Romania. It was abandoned in the reign of Aurelian.

Dromon: A fast single decked warship.

Dux (Duke): A senior Roman officer who commanded frontier forces.

Foederati (**federates**): Initially barbarian troops serving in the Roman army under their own leaders. By the sixth century they were regular units possibly recruited from barbarians, usually Germans.

Franks: A German people living along the lower Rhine who later took over France.

Gaul: The Roman name for an area including modern France, Belgium and parts of Germany west of the Rhine.

Gepids: An eastern Germanic tribe related to the Goths who remained beyond the Roman frontier. In the sixth century they fought against the Ostrogoths. Their name may be a pejorative derived from the Gothic word *gepanta*, meaning 'slow'.

Gruethungi: A third-fourth century Gothic clan.

Goths: The most powerful Germanic people in the third-fifth centuries who established two kingdoms inside the Roman Empire. The Visigoths, descended from the clans who crossed the Danube in 376, settled first in Western France and later moved into Spain. The Ostrogoths, who remained beyond the Roman frontiers until the late fifth century established a kingdom in Italy.

Heruls: An eastern Germanic people. They joined with the Goths in the third century to raid Greece and Asia Minor. Later, many served as mercenaries in the East Roman army against the Ostrogoths. They were noted for their light equipment and lack of armour.

Huns: A nomadic people from central Asia whose westward movements sparked off the Germanic migrations. Their warriors fought on horseback with bows.

Illyricum (Illyria): The Roman name for the area including modern Croatia and parts of the former Yugoslavia.

Isaurians: People from the Taurus mountains in modern southern Anatolia. These tough mountaineers became increasingly relied on by sixth century East Romans to man their armies. The Emperor Zeno was an Isaurian.

Legion (legio): By the fourth century a Roman legion was a unit of around 1,000 men who fought on foot with spears, javelins and swords.

Limes: The Roman frontier.

Limitanei: Second rate Roman troops who manned the frontier garrisons.

Lombards: A Germanic people who remained outside Roman territory until the sixth century. Many Lombards fought for the East Romans against the Ostrogoths and in 568 the Lombards moved into Italy to take it for themselves.

Magister Equitum **(Master of Horse):** One rank below the *Magister Militum* who theoretically commanded the cavalry but in reality led a mixed force. Therefore the *Magister Equitum intra Gallias* commanded the Gallic field army including both horse and foot.

Magister Militum **(Master of Soldiers):** The most senior Roman military commander below the Emperor.

Magister Peditum **(Master of Foot):** As above but theoretically commanding the foot. The *Magister Peditum Intra Italiam* commanded both horse and foot in the Italian field army.

Moors: The indigenous inhabitants of North Africa. Numbers of them fought as auxiliaries in the Roman army against the Ostrogoths. They were the ancestors of the modern Berbers.

Noricum: The Roman province roughly equating to parts of modern southern Bavaria, western Austria, and western Slovenia

Notitia Dignitatum: A list of offices and army units of the later Roman Empire

Ostrogoths: The branch of Goths descended from those who remained outside Roman territory in the fourth century and who followed Theodoric the Great into Italy at the end of the fifth century.

Palatini **(Palatine):** The most senior units of the late Roman field army.

Pannonia: The Roman name for the region of the middle Danube, before the bend, that includes parts of modern Austria, Hungary and Slovenia.

Rugians: An eastern Germanic tribe related to the Goths. Many of them were absorbed by Theodoric's Ostrogoths. In 554 the Rugian Eraric briefly ruled over both Rugians and Ostrogoths.

Sarmatians: A nomadic Iranian people who moved into the area beyond the Roman middle Danube frontier in the second century AD. They were famous for their heavy cavalry lancers.

Scirii: An eastern Germanic people who were absorbed by the Huns in the fifth century. After the collapse of the Hun Empire some were absorbed by the Goths, others struck out on their own and fought against the Ostrogoths. Odoacer was probably a Scirian.

Schola (pl. Scholae): Mounted guards units of the later Roman army.

Spangenhelm: A style of conical helmet formed of several pieces held together with reinforcing bands. It usually had a nasal guard, cheek pieces, and neck guard. The style probably originated amongst the Sarmatians along the Danube in the second century AD.

Suevi (also Suebi): A Germanic people, from modern Swabia. Many of them joined in the Vandal migration and settled in Spain until their destruction by the Visigoths. Others remained behind and fought against the Ostrogoths in the mid Fifth century.

Taifali (also Taifals): A barbarian tribe living in close proximity to the Goths in the third-fourth centuries. They may have been Germanic or possibly Sarmatian. They joined in the Gothic third century raids and a band of them linked up with some of the Goths who crossed the Danube in 376/7.

Tervingi: A third-fourth century Gothic clan which formed the bulk of the army which defeated the Romans at Adrianople in 378.

Visigoths: The branch of Goths descended from the followers of Alaric who ended up settling first in southwestern France and then in Spain.

Wielbark Culture: The name given by archeologists to the artefacts found in Pomerania which have been tentatively attributed to the early Goths.

Select Bibliography

Primary Sources

Ammianus Marcellinus, *Res Gestate.*
Annonymous, *Gallic Chronicle of 452.*
Cassius Dio, *Roman History.*
Cassiodorus, *Variae.*
Claudian, *On the Consulship of Stilicho.*
Dexippus, Publius Herennius. *Scythica.*
Gregory of Tours, *History of the Franks.*
Hydatius, *Chronicle.*
Isidore of Seville. *History of the Kings of the Goths, Vandals and Suebi.*
Jerome, *Chronicle.*
Jordanes, *Getica.*
Libanius, *Orations.*
Notitia Dignitatum.
Orosius, *History Against the Pagans.*
Olympiodorus, *Thebes.*
Paul the Deacon, *The Origin of the Lombard Nation.*
Priscus of Panium, *Fragments.*
Procopius, *History of the Wars.*
Prosper of Aquitaine, *Chronicle.*
Sidonius Appolinaris, *Poems and Letters.*
Strategikon of Maurice.
Tacitus, *Germania.*
Zosimus, *New History.*

Secondary Sources

Rather than an exhaustive list of every single work I have ever read, the following
sources are those I have found most useful in writing this book. I recommend all of
them to those readers who wish to learn more about the Goths and their impact on
the late Roman Empire.

Barbero, Alessandro. *The Day of the Barbarians.* (London, 2005)
Boss, Roy. *Justinian's Wars* (Stockport, 1993)
Bishop, Micheal C., and Coulston, Jon C N. *Roman Military Equipment from the Punic
    Wars to the Fall of Rome.* (London, 2006)
Burns, Thomas. *A History of the Ostrogoths.* (Bloomington, 1984)
Bury, J B., *The Invasion of Europe by the Barbarians.* (London, 1928)

Collins, Roger. *Visigothic Spain*. (Oxford, 2004)

Coombs-Hoar, Adrian. *Eagles in the Dust*. (Barnsley, 2015)

Delbrück, Hans. *The Barbarian Invasions*. Translated by Walter J Renfroe. (Nebraska, 1990)

Dixon, K and Southern, P. *The Roman Cavalry*. (London, 1992)

Drinkwater, J F and Elton, H. *Fifth-century Gaul: A Crisis of Identity*. (Cambridge, 1992)

Elton, Hugh. *Warfare in Roman Europe, AD 350-425*. (Oxford, 1996)

Gibbon, Edward. *The Decline and Fall of the Roman Empire*. (London 1777-88)

Goffart, Walter. *Barbarians and Romans*. (Princeton, 1980)

Goldsworthy, Adrian. *The Fall of the West*. (London, 2009)

Gordon, Colin Douglas. *The Age of Attila*. (Toronto, 1966)

Halsall, Guy. *Warfare and Society in the Barbarian West* 450-900. (2003)

— *Barbarian Migrations and the Roman West*. (Cambridge, 2007)

Heather, Peter. *Empires and Barbarians*. (London, 2009)

— *The Fall of the Roman Empire: A New History of Rome*. (Oxford, 2006)

— *Goths and Romans*. (Oxford 1991)

— *The Goths*. (Oxford, 1996)

Hodgkin, Thomas, *The Barbarian Invasions of the Roman Empire, Vol I The Visigothic Invasion*. (London 1880, reprinted 2000)

— *Vol III The Ostrogoths*. (London 1885, reprinted 2001)

Hoffmann, Deitrich. *Das Spaetroemische Bewegungsheer und die Notitia Dignitatum*. (Düsseldorf, 1970)

Hughes, Ian. *Stilicho, The Vandal Who Saved Rome*. (Barnsley, 2010)

Lot, Ferdinand. *The End of the Ancient World and the Beginning of the Middle Ages*. (Paris, 1939)

Jones, A H M. *The Late Roman Empire 284-602: Social, Economic and Administrative Survey*. (Oxford, 1964)

Junkelmann, M. *Die Reiter Roms*. (Mainz, 1993)

Kulikowski, Michael. *Late Roman Spain and its Cities*. (Baltimore, 2004)

— *Rome's Gothic Wars*. (Cambridge, 2008)

Luttwark, E.N. *The Grand Strategy of the Roman Empire*. (London, 1976)

MacDowall, Simon. *The Battle of Adrianople*. (Oxford, 2000)

— *Catalaunian Fields*. (Oxford, 2015)

— *Germanic Warrior*. (Oxford, 1996)

— *Late Roman Cavalryman*. (Oxford, 1995)

— *Late Roman Infantryman*. (Oxford, 1994)

— *The Vandals*. (Barnsley, 2016)

Mathisen, Ralph W and Shanzer, Danuta. *The Battle of Vouillé, 507 CE: Where France Began*. (Berlin, 2012)

Muhlberger, Stephen. *The Fifth-Century Chroniclers: Prosper, Hydatius, and the Gallic Chronicler of 452*. (Cambridge 1981).

Oman, Charles. *The Art of War in the Middle Ages*. (Oxford, 1885)

Thompson, Edward A. *Romans and Barbarians: The Decline of the Western Empire.* (Madison, 1982)

Ueda-Sarson, Luke. *The Notitia Dignitatum.* http://www.ne.jp/asahi/luke/ueda-sarson/

Wallace-Hadrill, John M. *The Barbarian West 400-1000.* (Oxford, 1967)

Wolfram, Herwig. (translator)Thomas J Dunlap. *History of the Goths.* (University of California Press, 1990)

Index